CATCHING CONFETTI

DEVELOPING THE MINDSET
OF A CHAMPION

Bret Burchard and Chris McAlister

Copyright © 2020 SightShift Publishing, LLC

Catching Confetti

———

Library of Congress Cataloging Data

Catching Confetti / Bret Burchard and Chris McAlister

ISBN: 978-1-7351070-0-4

———

Printed in the United States of America

For all the athletes, coaches, and ambitious people
who wish they had superpowers, but instead scratch and claw
for every step they take up the mountain.

This is for you.

To encourage you.

To help you relax and take a deep breath.

You're not crazy.

You can do it.

Keep climbing.

THANK YOU:

Chris for paving the way.

Tayler for pushing, cheering, and accompanying me on this climb.

Josh, Eric, Chris, Brandon, John, Eric, and Ingrid for sharpening the sword.

CONTENTS

INTRODUCTION

Ten seconds left.

Down 2.

Championship game.

The ball is in your hands.

Two minutes remaining.

No timeouts.

Need a touchdown.

Match point.

Finals.

Your serve.

Bottom of the 9th.

Bases loaded.

Full count.

When elite performers square off head-to-head the deciding factor is unseen to the novice eye. It's not technical skills or strategy. It's not strength or agility. It's not talent or prowess. When you face an opponent equal to you in skills, tactics, and strength, what gives you the edge?

Athletes and coaches at the highest levels invest excessive amounts of time, energy, and money developing technical skills and physical abilities. They hire world-class trainers, leave home at young ages to train with the best, and even neglect family responsibilities to master their craft. Fine-tuning swings and strokes. Innovating footwork and movement patterns. Training across disciplines and adopting strategies from around the world.

But what makes all of that preparation pay off when it matters most? What keeps the champions from caving when the pressure hits? When they do fail, how are they able to bounce back? When distractions come, what keeps them focused? When it seems like there is nothing left to accomplish, what motivates them?

Think of the athletic heroes you admire most. What is the difference maker that separates them from the rest? Is it Stephen Curry's form on his jump shot, or is it that he always seems to make the impossible ones? Is it Tom Brady's perfect spiral, or his game-winning drives in the final two minutes?

What captured the world's attention, Megan Rapinoe scoring more goals than anyone else in the 2019 World Cup, or that her vision transcended soccer? What made you call Michael Phelps the greatest of all time, his underwater dolphin kick, or that he won Olympic gold in every event he swam, and came one silver medal away from doing it again eight years after retiring?

The difference maker is mindset.

Most athletes, coaches, and leaders take a work harder approach to reach elite levels. It's true, you do need to work hard. There are plenty of people who haven't worked hard enough, who try to cheat the process, and aren't prepared for the moment. For those who do have the work ethic of a champion, there comes a point when your failures have less to do with your physical or tactical deficiencies and more to do with your mindset in the moment. It's a situation no amount of practice can protect you from. Working harder won't move the needle far enough if you neglect developing your mindset. How much time, money, and energy are you investing in developing yours? Do you dabble in the latest personal growth fads with unsatisfying results? Or are you leaving the development of your mental skills to chance, hoping you will figure it out as you age?

Society is advancing. Mental health awareness is increasing and more people are adopting strategies to help navigate difficult emotions. Schools are implementing yoga practice to improve study habits and attention spans. Organizations are teaching mindfulness in their employee development. Yoga and meditation are becoming mainstream performance hacks.

This is all good. Mindfulness matters. It is helpful to recognize when you feel certain emotions. When you make three errors in a row you need to be aware of your elevated stress response. You need to be able to breathe and to be present. But it's just the first step. Mindfulness by itself is not enough if you're trying to climb the highest peaks. You have to take the bigger step by developing your mindset.

Mindfulness without mindset training is like learning what's in your bank account without knowing how to make more money. It fails to integrate what you learn from mindfulness into your actions. Access to biofeedback is at an all-time high, measuring breathing patterns, posture, and sleep habits. Soon, measuring brain waves will be as commonplace as measuring your heart rate or taking your temperature. As you increase the awareness of your mindfulness, learn to upgrade your mindset too.

You lose three games in a row. Be mindful of the pain you feel. Upgrade your mindset to answer the challenge of regaining your composure.

You win five games in a row and begin to lose your vigilance. Mindfulness is being aware of the emotional change. Mindset is recovering the lost edge.

You hit a flow state. Mindfulness is recognizing you lost it. How do you recover it on demand? Mindset.

Your mindset determines how you perform in a match, from possession to possession; during a season, from game-to-game; and throughout your career, from year-to-year and through all phases. Your ability to develop your mindset will determine your potential to reach undiscovered heights and sustain success over time.

After more than a decade of studying the leading voices in human development, engaging in the most sought-after performance hacks, and working with elite athletes and business leaders, we have identified seven mindsets that, if developed, turn the greats into world-class. This book will teach you a new framework through which to view your life, your pursuits, and your relationships that will help you remove distractions and relax under pressure. It will guide you through simple practices and transformational experiences to actively develop the seven essential mindsets and position yourself for optimal performance state.

We will relate to your performance in sports and competition because we know you care so much about it. As we do, you will realize the transformation you have on the field or court will bleed over into the rest of your life. The mindsets elite athletes use to perform at world-class levels are the same mindsets you can use at home or work to build a life you enjoy and thrive in.

You won't develop all seven mindsets in the time it takes to read this book. Your sheer willpower won't flip your mental approach in a day. It takes time and consistent practice. The more you invest, the more you will improve, and the more you will keep improving with each new experience. Spend a week on each mindset. Read the chapter and then practice the exercises before moving on to the next. Each mindset will build on the previous ones and your development will continue to evolve long after you finish the book.

Most self-help books inspire you for a moment and then are forgotten. The hype eventually fades. This book has the potential to become an endless well of truth and encouragement for you. It will challenge you to dig deep below the surface of your desires, fears, and experiences. It won't always feel warm and fuzzy. It will demand heavy introspection. But the more you embody these practices and mindsets, the more insight you will discover. The further you go, the more transformational the change. Read through the book once and then reread it with a profounder understanding of who you are. Pick it back up for new applications as the seasons in your life change.

You already have everything you need to be the champion you desire. You just need to unblock the full expression of those elite qualities. When you do, you will no longer be left standing in awe of the heroes you see on TV and pay money to watch. You will become one yourself.

Runners, take your mark. It's time to tap into the hidden skill of mindset and watch the confetti rain on everything you've been trying so hard to achieve.

RESILIENT MINDSET

The ability to persevere regardless of the circumstances. The ability to separate who you are from your results. When your identity is not determined by your performance you can stand up under the pressure.

It was Thanksgiving morning. I woke up in sunny Phoenix, Ariz., to the smell of turkey and a holiday feast. My wife was cooking for her entire family to enjoy later that day. Our dog, tail wagging, begged for a portion. I packed my bags and headed for the airport, off to Sioux Falls, S.D., for the holiday weekend. I was the head coach of the Northern Arizona Suns, the minor league affiliate of the Phoenix Suns, and we were scheduled to play a Friday-Saturday back-to-back against the Sioux Falls Skyforce. Our Thanksgiving meal was catered that evening by the Sheraton in the hotel lobby.

On Friday we faced off against the Skyforce, only our second true road game of the season. We lost by 14 points. It was a learning experience for our young team and a game we thought we could build on. Our staff huddled early Saturday morning to come up with a game plan for the second night. The team who loses the first game usually has the edge in the second. We had adjustments to make while they would double down on what worked the first time. We were hungry for revenge while they were comfortable that they had the better team. Our starting center returned from injury and we had an NBA player on assignment. We entered Saturday's game with a plan of attack and a fighter's chance.

We lost by 35 points.

I was defeated.

It felt like a repeat of my first season as head coach. We tried every scheme and counter-attack in the book and managed just a 12-38 record. Now, halfway through this season, on a four-game losing streak, I saw the same story unfolding. There was little I could do to make up for our shortcomings.

What I realized later is my feeling of defeat was seeded from the beginning of the season. After a poor first season as head coach, I intended to show the rest of the league how much I learned and how much I improved. The clearest way to do that was to win more games in the second season. In my mind, more wins would vault me to a prominent role with an NBA team. This was the launching pad for the rest of my career. That 35-point loss made it clear we wouldn't win enough games for me to be validated.

Furthermore, we had four months remaining in the season and 42 more games to play. Now it was about survival. Quitting wasn't an option. We had to find a way to keep going. With my contract expiring at the end of the season, I had to find a way to coach without the threat of losing my job shutting me down. I had to coach with the patience, creativity, and boldness as if I had just signed a three-year contract extension.

With an advanced mindset, you can create a reality that doesn't exist to meet the reality of the moment. A Resilient Mindset is the catalyst that produces the courageous performances of our heroes. It's the reason you can get back up after a hard fall. It's the reason you can be at your best in the highest-pressure moments. It's the reason you can keep going regardless of the results.

> **A RESILIENT MINDSET IS GAINED IN THE TRENCHES, NOT MAGICALLY UNVEILED IN THE HIGHLIGHT REELS.**

You have to prepare for those moments, though. A Resilient Mindset isn't innate. It is gained in the trenches. It is not magically unveiled in the highlight reels. It is cultivated in the 10,000 small moments that make you want to quit. It is tested in the dark days of preparation and strengthened in the unseen work. That unseen work begins with a strengthening of the core of who you are: your identity.

A NEW FILTER

Before we go further let's unpack the word "identity". How you understand identity will have implications for each mindset explored in this book. Current popular culture tends to take one marker about who you are – whether it's race, ethnicity, sexuality, or in our case, a particular sport – and make it all of who you are. They magnify one marker, and in the process, neglect all of the other experiences and characteristics that make you who you truly are. Identity is bigger than any single marker. Maya Angelou said it best: "I do not represent blacks or tall women, or women or Sonomans or Californians or Americans. Or rather I hope I do, because I am all those things. But that is not all that I am."

Who you are, your identity, is more than the sum of your traits and experiences. To develop the Resilient Mindset, begin seeing your life through a new filter consisting of three components: your identity, your mission, and your community. Your identity is who you are. You will gain a deeper

IDENTITY > MISSION > COMMUNITY

understanding of this as you do progress through the book.

Your mission is what you do. It is your pursuit and the roles you fill. It is your performance and the results you seek. You swim, run, golf. You start or come off the bench. You seek first place or the varsity team. You're a teammate, employee, friend, child, parent, daughter, or son.

Third is your community or your relationships. It is your belonging and your acceptance within the groups you desire to be a part of. You have a team, a family, friendships, marriage, etc.

The fragility of your mindset comes when your identity is entangled with your mission and your community. Most people view their lives through mission or community first. You are a basketball coach. You are a golfer. You play for the University of _____. You are a mother. You are a son.

When who you are rests on the results of your performance or the relationships you have, you compete on unstable ground. You get to choose what you are defined by. If you build your identity around anything that can be gained or lost you set yourself up for crisis. You will develop a more Resilient Mindset by strengthening the core of who you are apart from what you do and who you are in relationship with. Focus on the security of your identity first.

ROOT OVER FRUIT

As I grew as a basketball player, I developed a hitch in my shooting stroke. Every coach through junior high and high school pointed it out and tried to correct it. They told me to stop pausing before I released it. They told me to "shoot all in one motion." Their advice became a broken record. I could see the hitch on video, but I couldn't feel it and I didn't know how to fix it. Telling me I had a hitch in my shot wasn't helping me. Trying to "shoot all in one motion" wasn't fixing the problem. I became frustrated with the whole skill.

> **WHEN YOUR FOUNDATION IS WEAK, YOU WON'T BE ABLE TO DEAL WITH LIFE'S STRESS AND PRESSURE APPROPRIATELY.**

Then I went to college and worked with a shooting coach named Jim Irwin. He was an experienced coach who had dedicated his work to studying the art of shooting. After watching me shoot for a while, he moved me closer to the basket and instructed me to relax my wrist. I was hyper-extending it, which threw off my timing and created the hitch in my release. As I learned to relax my wrist the rest of my stroke became smooth. Every other coach noticed the fruit that my mechanics produced – a hitch in my release. Coach Irwin addressed the root of the problem by relaxing my wrist. Once he transformed the root it created a lasting change in the fruit. The hitch was gone.

When you gloss over the impact of identity in any part of your life, you bypass the root of your development. When you focus on the fruit of your problems, you fail to make a lasting, transformational change. You might be able to will your way to temporary success, but eventually, you will crumble. As your foundation is eroded, you won't just cave under the biggest moments of stress, you will stumble under the smallest bits of pressure too. When your foundation is weak, you won't be able to deal with life's stress and pressure appropriately. Little moments of setback will throw you off balance. Small and big losses will evoke defensive outbursts. Mistakes will accumulate as you scramble to regain your footing.

Thousands of years of evolutionary biology have conditioned people to believe if we don't contribute, if we make a mistake, or if they don't like us, we will be shunned by the team and we won't eat. As the money involved in athletics has increased, the pressure to win has increased at all levels. You fall into believing the narrative that you have to win at all costs because you view your life and your peers' lives through the lens of mission and community. You convince yourself that if you just win enough then you will have security, whether that's job security, financial security, or security in belonging. The problem is it's not enough to win. You have to win the "Big One". And winning just one may not be enough either.

At some point, our greatest athletic heroes seem to always fall. Whether it's a meltdown under stress, a slip of the tongue, or an error in judgment in their social lives. Novices say that's just the risk you take when pushing to the edge of your abilities. The harder you push the boundaries the more likely you are to cross that proverbial line. Experts know that no amount of success will make them feel whole, so they learn to develop the core of their identity.

When you learn to separate who you are from what you do, the rest of your life will not hinge on your successes or failures.

BREAKDOWNS BECOME BREAKTHROUGHS

So how do you develop an identity that isn't crushed by a 35-point defeat? How do you develop a mindset that moves you forward after a season-ending injury, being demoted to a reserve role, or missing the cut?

You don't need to wait for the all-or-nothing moments to discover a misplaced identity. You don't need to experience them over and over until you hopefully develop a Resilient Mindset. Stress, whether real or imagined, reveals the weaknesses in your core. If you did a squat in the weight room with a 10-pound barbell, you could probably execute it with perfect form. Continue to load the bar with heavier weight and eventually your form will deteriorate. Your quads will shake and your knees will turn inward. Your body will compensate for areas you are weak in. The stress reveals where you need to improve to excel with heavier weights.

The same is happening for you internally. When your frustration escalates after consecutive mistakes, or when you lash out in anger after a loss, stress is revealing the insecurity of your identity. You can prepare for the stress of these situations by utilizing your imagination. Your brain doesn't decipher between what is real and what is imaginary. Have you ever awakened from a dream feeling guilty or terrified and had to convince yourself it wasn't real? Everything the brain experiences seems real. Use your imagination to experience stressful moments before they happen and surface areas of weakness in your core.

Before entering battle, samurai warriors imagined their death. It sounds counterintuitive. Sport psychologists would have advised them to imagine the perfect routine, the moment of glory, and the celebration afterward. There is a time and place for that kind of visualization, but recall our identity-first filter. That kind of visualization is based on performance. It is focused on mission and community. If you have to succeed to be welcomed back to the tribe and to see your family, then you have a lot to lose. You will fight with fear and hesitation. If you can be OK with dying, then you can fight with no fear. If you, as a coach or athlete, can see through to the other side of your death (i.e. losing a game, getting fired, or making a critical error) and see that your identity is still intact, then you can play and coach to the edge of your abilities without inhibition.

Phil Jackson was the head coach of the Chicago Bulls during the Michael Jordan and Scottie Pippen dynasty. In 1998, the Bulls were pursuing their third consecutive NBA title and sixth in eight years. During the Eastern Conference Finals, they faced a decisive Game 7 against the Indiana Pacers. In the days leading up to the game, Jackson told his team, "You have to face the possibility that you could lose a game like this."

You don't develop a Resilient Mindset by guaranteeing positive results. A Resilient Mindset is the ability to persevere regardless of the results. Use your imagination to strengthen your identity apart from the results of your performance so you can withstand the stress and compete with no fear or hesitation.

Close your eyes and imagine the worst possible outcome for whatever it is you are pursuing. You miss the shot, drop the ball, or get cut. You stutter through the presentation, get lost on the way to your interview, or miss the bus. Follow the trail of consequences because of your performance. What happens to you? Your career ends, you lose all your money, your partner leaves you. One season, as our team was in a tailspin, an assistant coach projected his ill fate and lamented, "I'm going to have to give back the Lexus!"

In your imagination, after all the terrible things happen and you reach the end of the rope, look at yourself in the mirror. Who are you? When everything you are attaching yourself to is stripped away, who are you?

You can imagine the positive outcome too, but don't stop at the results.

Continue the story down the trail of rewards for your winning performance: the fame, recognition, and accolades; the cash bonus or winning purse; the pension and retirement plan. Then return to the mirror. Who are you then?

If how you see yourself at the end of each of these stories is drastically different, then it's a clue that your identity is too intertwined with your performance or your relationships. This doesn't mean you have to feel happy about losing or sad when you win. Look deeper at your core. Who you are, your identity, is no more than or less than, no matter the outcomes.

The purpose of imagining the negative is not to beat yourself down until you are numb to the pain of failure. Later, you'll learn how emotions and feelings are the fuel to be utilized for your growth. This exercise is about surfacing where your identity is entangled with your mission and community. You can't completely ignore the possibility of experiencing adversity. You will face obstacles that you have to overcome, even if it's just a bad referee or stumbling out of the blocks. It's normal to hurt after a loss or mistake, but it's deflating to turn one mistake into many and self-sabotage. Resilience means you can re-engage no matter how big or how small the setback.

> YOU WILL FACE OBSTACLES. RESILIENCE MEANS YOU CAN RE-ENGAGE NO MATTER HOW BIG OR HOW SMALL THE SETBACK.

This isn't a one-time experience. As you keep stretching yourself to the edge of your abilities, you will experience moments when you want to quit. The non-resilient part of you will seek a pity party, highlighting the uniqueness of your struggle and building a case for why you have it harder than anyone else. It will fight and resist what the situation demands, hoping to achieve your goals without struggling through the hardest parts of the climb. When you feel this pain of inadequacy, big or small, it doesn't mean something is wrong with you. It means you are human on the path to mastery. Don't quit. Those feelings don't define you. On the other side of your struggle is a beautiful breakthrough, but you have to keep going to experience it. Solidify the core of who you are so you are prepared to stand up in the highest-pressure moments and, regardless of what happens, remain standing.

PRESSURE IS A MENTAL CONSTRUCT. WHEN YOU FEEL THE WEIGHT OF PRESSURE, YOU FALSELY BELIEVE WHO YOU ARE IS ON THE LINE.

THE LIE OF PRESSURE

This resiliency in mindset will set you on a trajectory towards greatness, but eventually, you will have to deliver in the biggest moments. The athletes who perform well under pressure don't feel the pressure. Not because they are superhuman. Not because they were born with a special gift that you will never have. Instead, during their careers, they learned a powerful secret.

Pressure is a mental construct. It is manufactured. When you feel the weight of pressure, you falsely believe who you are is on the line. You make a fatal mental error believing any one moment carries the weight to crush you. If this moment could be the "death" of you, that's too much weight to handle. No one can hold up under that amount of pressure for long. You might make short-term gains, but you won't sustain world-class performance. Clutch athletes have a mindset that transcends the results and outcomes. You may make a mistake. You may fail. But YOU are not a failure. Your identity is not outside of you. Who you are remains whole, regardless of the outcome.

This may be difficult to accept because it feels like there is a lot on the line. That is the secret, crippling power of pressure. It feels like the results carry astronomical significance, even when you can reason that it's "just a game." This is why it is important to practice developing a Resilient Mindset regularly. When you learn to separate who you are from the results of your performance, your brain won't interpret these moments with the pressure everyone else tries to impose on it. You will feel the excitement of showing up as your best self. When pressure arises, even if it comes unexpectedly, you will be prepared to reframe the moment through your identity first and position yourself to make the next right play.

Growing up, NBA Hall of Famer Kobe Bryant played in the Sonny Hill League, a summer basketball league in Philadelphia. His first year playing in the league, 11-year-old Kobe didn't score a single point the entire summer. Not a free throw, not a layup, not a lucky bounce. He was devastated. His father, a legend in the same league, hugged him and said, "Whether you score zero or score 60, I'm going to love you no matter what."

Kobe said it gave him all the confidence in the world to fail. With his identity assured, he thought, "To hell with that, I'm scoring 60. Let's go."

It is possible to have a Resilient Mindset in some areas more than others. Maybe you plow through setbacks at work, but obstacles at home send your relationships into chaos. Maybe you are nimble and charming when navigating relationships, but angry and vengeful with unexpected changes in your finances. You don't have to settle for specializing in one area. The same mindset you have in your athletic pursuits can be transferred to home or the corporate world as well. The key is to notice where you are seeking validation over growth. Are you blaming your coach, your partner, or an outside force? That's a caution flag for an inferior mindset. Life isn't fair. What will you do about it? Feel the security of who you are regardless of the circumstances and outcomes, and then take your best swing, relaxed with the pressure.

EXERCISES TO DEVELOP A RESILIENT MINDSET

1. Reframe Your Life

Reframe your life through an identity-first filter. Who are you apart from what you do and the relationships you have? If you're struggling with this, know that it's easier to figure out who you are by understanding who you are not. The following chapters will help you strip away any false identity you have built. Let's start by deciphering between identity, mission, and community.

In the first column, write out what you are pursuing (i.e. varsity team, first place, promotion) and the roles you fulfill (i.e. starter, reserve, teammate, child, parent). This is your mission.

In the second column, list the relationships you have and the groups you desire to belong to. This includes your team, family, social groups, or romantic partnership. These make up your community.

MISSION   COMMUNITY

_____   _____

_____   _____

_____   _____

_____   _____

_____   _____

2. Scenario Switching

Use your imagination to relive a pressure moment from your past or prepare for an upcoming one. Imagine the failure in this situation. Follow the trail of consequences until you reach the end of your rope. Then look at yourself in the mirror. Who are you?

Imagine the success in this situation, too. Look beyond the result to who you become because of it. Go back to the mirror. Who are you? Use this exercise to untangle your identity from your mission and community.

MINDSET 2

RELAXED MINDSET

———

Relaxed internally. A non-anxious presence. Nothing to prove, nothing to hide. Bringing your authentic self to the competition with confidence and humility.

In February 2020, Deontay Wilder and Tyson Fury squared off in what pundits called the most anticipated championship boxing match in a generation. It was a rematch of their first meeting that controversially ended in a draw. Both fighters were undefeated. Fury, the challenger, had 29 wins to his record and 20 knockouts. Wilder, the reigning champ and slight favorite, had 42 wins, 41 of them by knockout. He was known for his power hitting. The rematch sold over 1 million pay-per-view buys and set a gate record for ticket sales at the MGM in Las Vegas.

Cameras followed both fighters throughout the event, from arriving at the arena, through their pre-match routines, and eventually the walk to the ring. Wilder made his way to the arena through the casino with an entourage of family, coaches, and security. Everyone was straight-faced and somber-looking. The images of Wilder in his locker room before the fight showed him intensely pacing back-and-forth, methodically stretching, and carefully taping his hands. He stood eye-to-eye with his manager, receiving last-minute instructions and reminders. He sparred with a trainer.

Fury, on the other hand, had a police escort through downtown Las Vegas to the MGM. In the locker room, he was lounging on a leather couch watching TV. He smiled and winked at the camera. He danced, sang, and laughed with his team. It was uncomfortably close to the start of the match. I became nervous for him that he wasn't taking this serious enough.

For their walk to the ring, Wilder paraded down the ramp in a 45-pound suit of armor, full face-mask, and all. Fury was carried to the ring on an oversized throne, playing to his nickname, Gypsy King. While parading down the ramp he sang along to Patsy Cline's "Crazy" that was being blasted throughout the arena.

I knew you'd love me as long as you wanted,
And then someday, you'd leave me for somebody new.

Worry, why do I let myself worry?

Wondering, what in the world did I do?

Fury went on to win the fight when Wilder's corner threw in the towel midway through the seventh round. Afterward, Wilder complained that his legs were tired before the match even started because of the weight of his ring walk costume. Wilder's preparation for the fight appeared full of tension and anxious energy. Fury, on the other hand, seemed to be relaxed.

RELAXED DOES NOT MEAN LAZY

You may bristle at the idea of having a Relaxed Mindset. After all, you are known for your hard work and dedication. It's the reason you have made it this far. You pride yourself on taking no days off. You may have been inspired by the mantra, "If I'm not working then my competition is."

There is a difference between working hard towards a noble goal and insecurely seeking approval from your mission or community. Sharing 2 a.m. workout photos screams for attention and validation. Working late at night because it's the only available training time after you put the kids to bed hints at your dedication. Bragging about training while on vacation doesn't mean you are more committed. It may mean you mistakenly don't value the benefits of strategic rest. Sure, every great performer has a story of intense training seasons. You only hear about those because the recovery seasons make for a boring headline. Taking time to recover can help you achieve the performance you're training for more than you realize.

Having a Relaxed Mindset is not about being lazy. There's no doubt Tyson Fury had to work hard to become the heavyweight champion of the world. A Relaxed Mindset is about the presence you bring. It's about being relaxed internally. When your identity isn't on the line, you can engage with a non-anxious presence. You can wisely step away and recharge without feeling like you're falling behind. You can turn up your intensity when needed, but it's not out of your control. You won't need to force your will on the moment to be perceived a certain way.

To develop the Relaxed Mindset, you first need to understand what is happening underneath your anxious presence. Breathing exercises may calm the nerves for a moment, but it only covers up what is eating away at your core. You need to dig to the root of the anxiousness. Internally, there is a fear narrative driving your actions more than you realize. It's not just being afraid of the moment. It's the fear of what that moment could do to you. This fear clouds your mind's ability to reframe the moment through an identity-first filter. It makes you tense and disrupts the relaxed presence you need to engage the moment instinctively. One error becomes an indictment on your worth, so you consciously try harder the next time, but micromanaging your mechanics leads to more mistakes. You perform at your best when you surrender your skills to instincts and trust your training. Fear betrays that trust.

Everyone is grappling with this subconscious fear. Some are motivated by their fear in an unhealthy way and are marching to their eventual fall. Others are giving in to it every day. The great ones, whether they recognize it or not, have learned to process their fear through the filter of identity, which allows them to dance with pressure. The most advanced have learned to make peace with past experiences that introduced those fears and are no longer unconsciously driven by false motives. Before you learn how to create new experiences to propel yourself forward, you must first learn how to recognize when fear is exerting its control.

> YOU PERFORM AT YOUR BEST WHEN YOU SURRENDER YOUR SKILLS TO INSTINCTS.

PROVING AND HIDING

I remember sitting in the dentist's chair for a routine cleaning. The hygienist laid the chair back and told me to open wide. She selected multiple sharp objects and began poking at sensitive spots in my mouth. She tried to distract me with a TV but I couldn't watch it. There was a much more dangerous situation at hand. All of my attention was on the tools threatening to inflict pain on my gums and those beady eyes staring at me through two layers of magnifying glasses. I was skeptical of her intentions.

During a pause in her work, I turned my attention away from the operation. I noticed my entire body was clenched. Toes curled under, quads flexed, back tightened, fingers gripping the armrests. I was in full defensive mode. Without me even realizing it, my brain felt the threat and triggered my body into a protective posture.

The same happens to us emotionally. When you feel threatened in your identity, you will unconsciously protect yourself against vulnerability. Your brain's defense mechanism is to prove or to hide. When you hide, you shrink back and diminish your contributions to the team. You remove yourself from the edge of your abilities for fear of being exposed for who you truly are. Alternatively, proving is seen in the unnecessary increases of intensity. When you feel your identity attacked, you power up or shout louder with your words or actions to be seen and heard. What you try so hard to show everyone else is the precise thing you don't believe about yourself.

As an assistant coach for the Phoenix Suns, I worked with a first-round draft pick during his rookie season. He was a blue-chip prospect who came from a premier college basketball program. To stick in the NBA, though, he needed to improve his shooting. During the offseason, we planned to rework the mechanics of his jump shot, arriving early to the practice gym before anyone else. We were doing basic-level drills to reprogram his biomechanics. It was just me and him in the gym. As long as we were alone, he was fully engaged. As soon as another person walked into the gym, he quit working. He left to go to the bathroom or asked to do a different drill that was more aligned with his strengths. He didn't want to be seen being coached. His insecurity told him that if he was being coached that meant he was not good enough. He lived with an anxious presence, always checking the sidelines to see who was judging. As a result, he became the person he feared. When his teammates engaged in post-practice shooting competitions, he declined to participate. Instead, he watched from the sidelines, talking trash when they missed. His identity couldn't handle the prospect of being exposed as inadequate. The vulnerability triggered his brain to protect him by hiding from the moment.

If you're only motivated to prove your worth or belonging, then you will have to continually stir up discontent. You won't compete from a place of overflow and joy. You will compete only to get what you need in your identity. If your tendency is to hide, you may not participate at all. That chip on your shoulder may have helped you survive in the past, it may have pushed you further than anyone else, but it won't take you as far as you're capable. Eventually, it works against you. When you are proving and hiding, the only way you can relax is if "they" give you an indication that they see you and acknowledge you. As you try to take that from them, they will push you away. As you seek approval, you miss opportunities to grow. You power up more, or go further into hiding, until you reach your demise. To play at your highest capacity, you need to lose the chip on your shoulder and relax into who you are.

To be clear, the need to produce results is different than the need to produce an identity. The players I coached in the NBA G League felt every day they had to prove they were worthy of a call-up to the NBA. This bit of stress heightened their focus each day. They needed to produce results to earn a spot in the big leagues or else the organization looked for a different player. The athletes who positively impacted the outcomes earned the call-ups. The athletes who tried to show off and impress didn't.

SHOW UP TO IMPACT, NOT IMPRESS.

Train yourself to be the kind of person who impacts by recognizing when you are proving and hiding. If you can recognize it in the smallest, insignificant moments, you will be prepared for the biggest, high-pressure moments. Start by recalling situations when you felt unusually stirred up. Maybe you became angry over a trivial event or wanted to run away and escape. How did you feel threatened as it related to your identity? You can reflect at the end of each day or replay intense moments after they arise. Eventually, you will notice proving and hiding as it's happening. The real superpower is being able to redirect the urge to prove and hide into a relaxed engagement. This level of athleticism takes a deeper understanding of the precise fear that is driving your life right now.

IDENTITY FEARS

There are two kinds of fear. There is a legitimate fear of physical danger. When you hunker down in the basement because there is a tornado outside, that is a legitimate fear. There is also the fear of shame. It's a fear everyone struggles with, whether they realize it or not. It's different than guilt. Guilt is feeling bad about what you have done. Shame is feeling bad about who you are. Shame communicates a lie about who you are and fear makes you feel that lie.

What follows is a description of nine foundational identity fears. The reason you prove and hide is to protect yourself from these feelings of fear. When you know your identity is not defined by what you do or who you are in relationship with, you don't have to be driven by the false threat of shame. Examining these fears can be uncomfortable. You may see parts of yourself in each one or one may resonate more than others. What you are noticing is not a weakness. It's the clue to what triggers your anxious presence. Let them be a guide as you work to understand specifically why you are proving and hiding, and how you can counteract those responses.

FEAR OF NOT BEING NEEDED

The lie you believe: "If I'm not needed, then I'm not appreciated."

If this is your core fear, then your proving and hiding will be centered around making others realize they need you. You will find ways to keep everyone connected to you by embedding yourself as the one they depend on. If you are not the one they depend on, then you will overexert yourself to prove your status, or you will withdraw and smile when the team does poorly without

> SHAME COMMUNICATES A LIE ABOUT WHO YOU ARE AND FEAR MAKES YOU FEEL THAT LIE.

you. You won't accept another person taking the lead role if you feel like the supporting cast. You desperately want to organize the team around you and your abilities. For example, if you, as a coach, are driven by this fear, you might design a system to keep your athletes dependent on you. Because you don't empower them to make decisions autonomously, you stunt their development and creativity.

FEAR OF NOT BEING CARED FOR

The lie you believe: "If I don't take care of myself, no one else will."

If this is your core fear then you feel the weight of the world on your shoulders. There is no place you can go to rest and know that it will be ok. You feel trapped with no way out. Panicked, feeling like you're running out of options, you keep busy to distract yourself from the pain. Some athletes go to the gym because they love going to the gym. They love developing their skills, building confidence with repetitions, and pursuing mastery. You go to the gym to comfort your pain. You don't compete out of joy. You compete out of a misplaced hope that the thing you are chasing will be your savior. So, you manufacture ways to get there. You implement eight different training techniques. You try every new gimmick. You dive after every ball no matter how far out of reach. As a coach, you turn over stones that you have already turned over twice. Honestly, why are you re-watching that game for the fourth time? It's false hustle. You're searching for ways to ignore what you're truly feeling. The celebration and acceptance you are looking for is already inside you.

FEAR OF NOT BELONGING

The lie you believe: "I don't belong."

If this is your core fear, then you are constantly searching for the team, group, or role that you can call home. With each stop, you believe this will finally be the place you can be known for who you truly are. If this is your fear, then your proving and hiding will center around belonging. You will frequently reference the important people you are connected to or make those connections seem stronger than they are. Maybe you will hide in the corner and not engage so you can't be further pushed out. The people driven by this fear are searching for peace that they can't find within. You ignore problems or refuse to admit deficiencies because you would rather just fit in to feel at peace. You spend more energy pretending you don't have any deficiencies than you do working to improve your weaknesses.

FEAR OF INADEQUACY

The lie you believe: "I don't have what it takes."

You are so afraid to fail that you only focus your energy on what you know you can be exceptional at. If you can't perform flawlessly, then you won't try it. You hyper-specialize in one area, pouring all you have into it so no one can ever again say you don't have what it takes. You may be confident in your skills and expertise in your sport, but feel out of place when attempting home improvement projects. You may be great relating with teammates, but struggle to see the crossover in skills when relating to those outside your sport. Because you can't give yourself patience in new endeavors, you have a short leash with others when they try on new roles.

FEAR THAT GOOD ENOUGH IS NEVER GOOD ENOUGH

The lie you believe: "I can't perform well enough to feel worthy."

You constantly feel behind on the scoreboard. No matter what you achieve or how well you perform, it's never enough to make you feel satisfied with who you are. You might kill it with a record-setting performance, but that one bobbled ball will eat at you the rest of the week. Your team won by 20, but it could have been 22 if you managed the game better. You define your life by your performance in your work or relationships. You lead yourself and others with the presence of a driving taskmaster. You work yourself to death, needing more success and greater achievements.

Eventually, you will wear yourself and others out. You either keep coming up short or you feel the emptiness of achievement for achievement's sake. The next win is all that matters.

FEAR OF BEING A BAD PERSON

The lie you believe: "I am bad."

You believe you receive negative outcomes because you are a bad person. You settle for being treated poorly by a coach or administrator because you think you deserve it. Maybe you were mistreated by an influential person in your past who you expected to love and protect you. You believe the lie that is was your fault. You falsely believe coaching is just about being critical, so you constantly tear yourself and others down. Your results become a self-fulfilling prophecy.

FEAR OF A BAD OUTCOME

The lie you believe: "If I mess up, the worst will happen."

You are constantly afraid that one false step will bring your whole world crashing down. You struggle with anxiety, always waiting for the worst to happen. You power up and prove by micromanaging every variable, thinking you can control the results with a formula. If you follow the recipe then you will win. You hide behind a cause-and-effect worldview. Maybe it's an attachment to a superstition or a routine. You are looking for a guarantee, but there is never a guarantee in mission or community and it paralyzes you. The anxiety and self-doubt slow you down, causing you to move a half-step too slow.

FEAR OF VULNERABILITY

The lie you believe: "If I'm vulnerable, I'll be hurt."

There was a time in your life when you were vulnerable and it came back to bite you. Perhaps your talents as a youth prodigy were taken advantage of by adults and now you're not sure who to trust. Maybe you opened up about concerns within the organization and it cost you your job. The experiences hurt you deep enough that you have built walls to protect yourself from ever being hurt again. You throw your weight around to keep teammates and co-workers off balance and at arm's length. You reveal only the parts of you that can't be hurt. You play devil's advocate so you don't risk being exposed. You stay unpredictable so no one can truly know you. Your fear of vulnerability is keeping you from utilizing the greatest superpower in team building.

FEAR OF BEING REPLACEABLE

The lie you believe: "I'm not special."

You feel like you don't have a unique place within the team. You feel that your unique contributions are not appreciated or required. You believe no one notices your special gifts, so you find ways to test life and validate your fear. You stay quiet, waiting to be called on. You stand on the sideline waiting to be picked. If they don't ask for your participation, it's proof they don't value you. At your worst, you're not even sure they see you at all. Even if your locker is in the center of the room, you can't help but wonder if they would notice if you were gone. The feeling of being replaceable is suffocating. Accepting new teammates or losing your priority in the group freezes you. You impose stern discipline on yourself to stand out from the others. You tear down anyone else who might take your place. Inside, you are screaming to be seen and heard as unique.

As you reflect on the nine fears, don't feel pressure to fit yourself into one category. Focus on noticing proving and hiding first. Then try to connect those situations to a specific fear you may have been feeling in the moment.

Why did I become so angry when he didn't call me
before he went to the gym?

Because it made me feel that I wasn't needed,
and if I'm not needed then I'm not appreciated.

Why was I so hesitant to talk to anyone?
Because I didn't feel like I belonged.

Over time, one of these fears will emerge as a common theme in your life. You don't have to force a false story in haste. Later, you will learn how to flip these lies into truth that moves you forward, but first, you need to surface the lie and understand where it originated.

EXPERIENCES SHAPE YOU

Your life experiences don't define you but they do shape you. They have the power to unconsciously wedge these fear triggers into your psyche. It can happen through a thousand little stings over time, or there can be one dramatic moment that sticks with you forever.

In my second year as head coach of the Northern Arizona Suns, we were playing against the Texas Legends. Their arena was connected to an ice rink. As we were preparing for our game, a youth hockey tournament was taking place next door. Through the wall of our locker room, I overheard a dad talking to his son. It started as talking, then escalated to shouting.

"If you don't start skating harder, I'm going to tell the coach to take you out! You only skate hard when you have the puck! Your ice time will be determined by how hard you skate!"

It was a similar message I gave to professional players, but the delivery seemed a little aggressive for a child.

It continued. "This is playoff hockey! If you don't win, your season is over! It's time to man up!"

Man up? He's 10 years old.

Then the kill shot: "I'm sick of hauling your ass all over this state to watch you play like this!"

And just like that, to an impressionable child, a lie is wedged in his heart about how he sees himself.

My needs are a problem.

I must take care of myself, or no one else will.

The seed of false hustle is planted.

This has happened to each of us along our journey. Whether directly or indirectly, subtly or blatantly, painful experiences have introduced lies to your identity and triggered fear responses. Wrestling with these fears is not meant to make you feel bad about yourself. Reflecting on past experiences is not about assessing blame to people in your life or stirring up vengeful feelings. This entire process is about understanding what is happening internally so you can bring an authentic expression of yourself externally.

A MALLEABLE MIND

The more you are aware of your internal state, the less likely you will be overtaken by the emotions of any particular moment. A relaxed mind does not compete from a state of fear. With a Relaxed Mindset, you can turn up or turn down the volume of intensity as needed and compete with confidence and humility. You can direct your willpower to cooperate with the moment.

In his first season as head coach of the Phoenix Suns, Jeff Hornacek led a 48-win team and missed the playoffs by just one game. At halftime of a midseason contest, the Suns were losing and not playing well. The mild-mannered Coach Hornacek burst into the locker room, flailing his arms and shouting at each player to play harder and play tougher. It was one of those speeches that silences the locker room. Trainers stopped distributing water. Players stopped fidgeting with their uniforms. No one talked of strategy or tactics. The point was made.

When he left the locker room, Coach Hornacek looked at his assistant coaches with a grin and said, "We'll see if that works." Because he had a Relaxed Mindset, Coach Hornacek could quickly modulate between intense and calm as necessary. He wasn't overtaken by the moment. He gave the moment exactly what it needed.

There is a time to turn up the level of your intensity. There is also a time to take a deep breath and bring a calming presence to the activity. When your brain is not stressed by insecurity, it will be aware of the cues showing which one is needed for this moment.

Ambitious competitors struggle with the tension between confidence and humility. Being humble is an admirable virtue, but you can't survive at the top of the mountain without confidence. Those two qualities don't have to be mutually exclusive. It comes down to motive.

In the classic movie Hoosiers, small-town Hickory High School had the ball with a chance to upset the larger South Bend Central Bears for the Indiana State High School basketball championship. Coach Normal Dale drew up a game-winning play that used star player Jimmy Chitwood as a decoy. The entire team was stunned. Jimmy looked at his teammates, then at his coach, and delivered the movie's climactic line: "I'll make it."

Everyone knew Jimmy was the best player on the team. Earlier in the season, the town threatened to fire Coach Dale because Jimmy refused to play. Jimmy knew he was the best player on the team. He saved the coach's job by agreeing to join the team. Jimmy wasn't so insecure that he needed to have the play drawn up for him so he could be the hero. When he called for the ball on the last play, he was aware of what that moment needed and what skills he brought to the table. He delivered with humility and confidence.

You can have an unshakeable confidence in your abilities without hijacking the team to put your talent on display. You can have the humility to defer to teammates without shrinking back or hiding your desire to grow. You can play with a swagger that thrives in the biggest moments without seeking validation from others because of your performance. You can accept the role you are given without diminishing your contribution.

An anxious mind will always be tempted by the desire to force its will onto the situation or sit back and wait to be called on. You don't have to throw your hands up and passively resign to whatever happens. You also don't have to clench your fists and double down on discipline and harder work. Instead of fighting against what is happening, use willpower to participate with and accelerate what is happening. Your awareness of proving and hiding is the secret to living humble and confident.

In the first meeting between Wilder and Fury in 2018, the one that ended in a draw, Fury was knocked down twice but battled back to even the score. Many believe he won the fight aside from the two knockdowns. In the post-fight locker room, Fury displayed the malleability of the Relaxed Mindset. His team didn't dwell on the idea of being cheated out of a championship. There was no complaining or blaming. Fury told them, "Don't worry about it. Don't make a big deal of it. We know the truth. I won that fight." Within minutes after a split-draw decision, Fury had sealed the confidence he needed from the experience and turned his team's focus to a rematch he knew he could win.

The path to your pinnacle will have peaks and valleys. The peaks inspire you to start. The climb will try to knock

A RELAXED AND HARNESSED MIND IS THE MOST POWERFUL TOOL IN YOUR ARSENAL.

you off balance. You prepare for a successful climb in the valleys by solidifying your core to endure the hardships and navigate the terrain. A relaxed and harnessed mind is the most powerful tool in your arsenal. It brings a full, authentic expression of who you are, allows you to adjust to any circumstance, and allows you to keep growing through every new challenge you face.

EXERCISES TO DEVELOP A RELAXED MINDSET

1. Notice Proving and Hiding

Recall past experiences when you powered up to prove or withdrew and hid out of fear of being exposed. Consider times you overly displayed confidence or intentionally chose to act humble. We often confuse proving and hiding with false expressions of confidence and humility. Make it a daily practice to notice proving and hiding in the midst of intense competition or in the smallest moments at home or in the locker room.

2. Name Your Fear

Reread the nine identity fears. Which one do you resonate with the most? There may be more than one that stands out to you. Don't pressure yourself into finding "the one." As you become more aware of proving and hiding, patterns will emerge that are connected to your core fear. It will reveal itself.

MINDSET 3

VICTOR MINDSET

The ability to flip obstacles into opportunities and to create advantages out of your disadvantages. Understanding you are a work in progress, not a finished product. The Victor loves growing even more than winning.

Entering the 2018 USA 25k Championships, accomplished long-distance runner Sarah Crouch was plateauing. Despite winning races, it had been years since she ran anything close to her best times. She was losing hope that she could still improve. Before the race she said:

> This year I've raced quite a bit, but to be totally honest I haven't put myself into races where losing was very likely. It turns out that winning when you're not trying very hard isn't super satisfying. So, I'm actually here to kind of get my butt kicked a little bit.

Sarah Crouch has a Victor Mindset.

Josh Waitzkin was a child prodigy in chess and the subject of the 1993 movie Searching for Bobby Fischer. With an expert coach and a thorough training program, he became an International Master. With nothing left to accomplish in chess, he switched disciplines and became a world champion in martial arts. In his book, The Art of Learning, Josh said, "What I have realized is that what I am best at is not Tai Chi, and it is not chess – what I am best at is the art of learning." He went on to describe his process for becoming a master:

> Chess was a constant challenge. My whole career, my father and I searched out opponents who were a little stronger than me, so even as I dominated the scholastic circuit, losing was part of my regular experience. I believe this was important for maintaining a healthy perspective on the game. While there was a lot of pressure on my shoulders, fear of failure didn't move me so much as an

intense passion for the game.

Josh Waitzkin has a Victor Mindset.

In 2011, Lebron James was named an NBA All-Star for the seventh consecutive season, earned All-NBA First Team honors for the fifth time, and was voted to the NBA All-Defensive First Team for the third-straight time, but his Miami Heat lost the championship to the Dallas Mavericks. After the loss, he won two consecutive NBA titles and three in the next five years. Although he was already considered among the best players in the history of the league, he credits that 2011 series for making him even better:

> *I wasn't that good of a player in that series. I wasn't a complete basketball player. [Mavericks assistant coach] Dwane Casey drew up a game plan against me in that '11 series in the Finals when I played Dallas to take away things I was very good at and tried to make me do things I wasn't very good at. So, he's part of the reason why I am who I am today.*

Lebron James has a Victor Mindset.

After receiving backlash from a controversial Saturday Night Live skit, actress and comedian Tina Fey said:

> *I felt like a gymnast who did a very solid routine and broke her ankle on the landing…I have decided that a culture of apology is not for me, so what I do is I promise, anyone*

3

who is mad at me, I hear you, and I will learn and I will continue to change. But I'm also not going to stop trying. You have to be an athlete about it.

Tina Fey has a Victor Mindset.

The people who go the furthest have the mindset to continually seek opportunities to grow and then pursue that growth diligently. They seek out world-class coaching to show them what they don't already know, they have a deep motivation, and they practice diligently.

When you develop a Victor Mindset you become a craftsman in your field, a student of the game. A day in training is less about the result of your performance and more about what you learned. The hitter who whiffs five times in a row can crack his bat over his knee or he can pay attention to his mechanics and adjust to improve his chances. The obstacle to growth is not in the number of mistakes. It is in the mindset you bring to new challenges. Tiger Woods changed his golf swing multiple times throughout his career, even while winning major championships.

LIFE IS MORE ABOUT WHO YOU ARE BECOMING THAN WHAT YOU ACHIEVE.

Life is more about who you are becoming than what you achieve; more about learning and experiencing than conquering and accomplishing. You weren't the same five years ago that you are today and you won't be the same five years from now. You are a work in progress, not a finished product. If you're not growing then you're not experiencing the fullness of life.

The ability to grow means you have limitless potential. There is no ceiling because you can always evolve and improve. But in order to grow, you have to be challenged. You have to subject your abilities to a level of stress. You can't grow if you're coasting through life. You don't want to overload stress to the point you feel like you are drowning. Too much stress can pressure you to create negative patterns and take short cuts just to stay afloat. Instead, immerse yourself in conditions just challenging enough to stretch the edge of your abilities. With a Resilient Mindset, you can persevere in the face of failure. With a Victor Mindset, you flirt with failure.

To develop a Victor Mindset, learn to flip obstacles into opportunities and disadvantages into advantages, use mistakes for propulsion, and lean into moments of pain.

VICTOR MINDSET VS. VICTIM MINDSET

There is no easy path through life or to the pinnacle of your pursuit. You will face obstacles. You will experience hardships. Kobe Bryant described losing as exciting. "It means you have different ways to get better. There are certain things you can figure out, that you can take advantage of, certain weaknesses that were exposed that you need to shore up." For Kobe, weaknesses became opportunities to grow. Challenges became lessons.

Challenges can either grow you or distort you. When you view them through the broken mindset of a victim, they will deform you. If you view them through the mindset of a Victor, you will grow because of them.

A victim mindset sees obstacles through the lens of mission and community, an insecure identity that is defined by the results. It protects by proving and hiding. A Victor Mindset chooses to see the opportunities within each obstacle, knowing it will become greater because it went through the experience.

A victim mindset looks for an easier route to validate its awesomeness to the world. A Victor Mindset seeks out the challenges to sharpen the edges of its abilities.

A victim mindset gets swallowed up in pity, thinking life isn't fair. A Victor Mindset sees the difficult situation for what it will develop in them. A victim mindset focuses on the advantages of others. A Victor Mindset looks at the disadvantages and gets excited about the opportunity to flip it into an advantage.

During basketball practice with the Suns, we split the team into two groups, one group on each end of the court. We challenged each group with a shooting game. If they made the shot, it counted as one point for the players. If they missed the shot, it counted as one point for the coaches. First to 12 points won and we played five rounds, each from a different spot on the court. Both groups had opposite responses to the challenge.

On one end, the players made five consecutive shots and complained the game was too easy. They changed the rules and doubled the challenge. In their new rules, the coaches received two points for every miss instead of one. They won four out of the five rounds.

On the other end, the players were neck-and-neck with the coaches on the scoreboard. Rather than focusing on making the next shot to maintain their lead, they complained about the scorekeeping. They accused the coaches of miscounting. They dramatized how they had been cheated. They lost four out of the five rounds.

Victims contribute to their own demise, becoming distracted by uncontrollable elements and believing the world is against them.

Victors believe their efforts can make a difference in achieving results.

Victims spend more effort trying to save face when circumstances turn against them, hoping the results will validate them.

Victors love to grow, even more than they love to win.

LEAN IN

You aren't born with a Victor Mindset. It is cultivated over time. Like all soft skills, the Victor Mindset can be learned and developed. You may notice you have a Victor Mindset in certain areas more than others because of your experiences. The biggest challenge for Teddy Atlas was protecting his fighters from the trap of a victim mindset.

A legendary boxing trainer, Atlas is most famous for helping Michael Moorer defeat Evander Holyfield for the heavyweight championship in 1994. Moorer had a reputation for being a difficult student. He had the physical ability to win a title, but was moody and had bad training habits. He would walk out of training camps, refuse to spar, and drink too much. Leading up to a fight, Moorer would make a public spectacle of his lack of discipline. According to Atlas, Moorer was hedging his bets and looking for an excuse to lose. If he did lose, he had a reason other than he just wasn't good enough. He didn't have the guts to lose on his own. He was scared. To keep yourself from falling into the trap of a victim mindset, learn to lean into your fear.

Your subconscious mind communicates with your conscious mind through emotions and feelings. Paying attention to those feelings will give you valuable insight into where you can grow. Most tough competitors have been taught that emotions are a sign of weakness, so they stuff them down and don't let them show. Others have been taught to wear their emotions on their sleeves. Feel it and do it. Don't hold back. Both of these approaches are lies taught by insecure people. Advanced performers live in the tension of these two approaches. They feel their emotions deeply without denying them and without being dominated by them. The boxer in training sits in his hotel room late at night and feels the fear of potentially losing. He can notice the desire to hide from the moment without acting on it and abandoning his training regimen. He is aware and learning.

Stuffing down your emotions may rack up achievements in the short-term, but it silences the voice of your creative brilliance that can take you even further. Instead of listening to the messages of your feelings, you quiet the pain with addictions and compulsions. You numb out to the wisdom that points you to your next growth opportunity. Those addictions may be as destructive as drugs and alcohol, as innocent as social media and TV, or as noble as working harder. You use these vices to relieve yourself of the pain of the moment, whether it's a fear of failure faced far too many times, anxiety as you approach uncharted territory, or disappointment over another missed opportunity.

DON'T DENY YOUR EMOTIONS AND DON'T BE DOMINATED BY THEM. BE AWARE AND LEARN.

I worked with an NBA player on a non-guaranteed contract who refused to take a day off for fear of falling behind. He worked so hard he was urinating blood by the end of the season. He comforted his pain by going to the gym.

When sporting events were canceled and seasons postponed in 2020, players and coaches were forced to spend more time at home with their families. Many turned to busy work to avoid facing the uncomfortable new reality. Maybe you dive deeper into the details of game plans to avoid a vulnerable relational conversation with your athletes. You convince yourself the new schemes will give you a competitive advantage, but miss the real catalyst to strengthening your team.

The fear you feel is the lying voice of shame. Fortunately, shame is a terrible poker player. It tips its hand by standing precisely in the path of where you should go next. If you continue to give in to its hurdle, you will never reach your full potential. If you stop numbing out and follow the fear, it will lead you toward your greatest accomplishments.

The hype of self-help gurus says, "If you want to be great you have to be comfortable being uncomfortable." In my experience, being uncomfortable never becomes more comfortable. Fear never completely goes away. Every step of growth invites more fear. I was grateful when a fear-conquering expert affirmed my sentiment.

In mountain biking, fear is expressed through your hands. In the community I first rode with, it was shameful to squeeze the brakes with two fingers. Braking with more than one finger was a telltale sign of a novice rider.

Me? I used eight fingers. Four on the back wheel and four on the front wheel.

That is, of course, until I understood how fear was impacting my riding.

One spring I took my bike into the shop for a tune-up. The mechanic looked every part of a professional mountain biker. Straight-legged shorts reaching beyond his knees, form-fitting X-Games T-shirt, shaggy hair, and unkempt scruff on his face. I felt out of place wearing my high-top sneakers and basketball shorts.

As he took my bike to the back he asked me, "How do you like your brakes, tighter or looser?"

I told him, "I like them to work!"

I explained that I get scared on the downhills and squeeze my brakes hard, but I don't feel like they slow me down. My bike travels too fast around the curves and I can't steer it through the rocks and crevices. After inspecting my bike, he told me the brakes were working fine, then added sage-level wisdom, free of charge: "We all get scared. Once we conquer the fear on one trail we just start riding harder stuff."

I didn't need better brakes. I needed to recognize my fear and respond differently. Instead of allowing fear to dominate me into exerting more control over the bike, I needed to relax. Instead of hiding behind tighter brakes, I needed to lean into the contours of the trail and let the bike do the work. And when the fear dissipates, I'll know it will be time to start riding harder stuff.

The more you grow, the deeper you will experience fear. You don't have to be comfortable being afraid, but you do have to build a habit of leaning into your fear.

LEARN YOUR STORY

The stories of your triumphs begin with the moment you lean into fear and take a vulnerable risk. The stories of your disappointments hinge on moments when you shy away from fear to protect yourself from pain. Before you write the inspiring story of your future, deconstruct the stories of your past to understand you are not broken.

> THE MORE YOU GROW, THE DEEPER YOU WILL EXPERIENCE FEAR. BUILD A HABIT OF LEANING INTO YOUR FEAR.

As you saw with the hockey dad in the previous chapter, the fear you recognize now was amplified through a painful experience in your past. Children are great recorders, but terrible interpreters. When your dad said, "I'm sick of hauling your ass all over this state to watch you play like this," your child brain didn't think, "Dad is insecure because of how he was treated as a boy." Instead, your brain kicked into survival mode. At the time, you sped past those moments to cope with the pain. If you replay the tape in slow motion, you will become aware of how your brain introduced a narrative around your fear.

I need love.

*Dad expresses his love for me by taking
me to hockey games.*

*He doesn't enjoy watching me play
unless I skate hard.*

*If I don't work harder, he won't love me.
I must hustle hard to be loved.*

Because the brain can't handle dissonance, it forces this story on smaller moments throughout your life. Eventually, it becomes ingrained in the way you react to every pressure moment. You had a painful experience with failure before, so you will avoid steps that may lead to failure in the future. You were abandoned before, so you won't put yourself in a position to be abandoned again. You falsely believe you aren't capable, you don't add any value, or you won't be accepted even if you try because of the lies that were introduced in your past. To develop a Victor Mindset, you have to unlearn these patterns of survival.

Recall the most hurtful moments of your life. Even if they seem small and insignificant, pay attention to events that bother you the most and you wish your brain would forget. They bother you for a reason. What circumstances seem to repeat no matter which team you are on? There is probably a blind spot you refuse to acknowledge. You can continue to ignore it, you can blame others, or you can bring it to light and deal with it.

Replay these moments in your life in slow motion. Deconstruct them as carefully as you would deconstruct your footwork after a turnover or the alignment of players in a critical possession. How might these moments be connected to the core fear you learned about in the previous chapter? What lie did you believe that caused you to respond that way? Recalling these memories will help you discover where these false narratives originated. You don't have to build your identity around the hardships that happened to you. They may have shaped parts of your identity, but they are not your whole identity. You don't have to hide behind the obstacles your story has created.

It's normal to have challenges. You don't have to be a victim, completely taking your hands off the handlebars. You also don't have to fight for your dignity. Gripping the handlebars tighter and throwing your willpower behind broken strategies is self-sabotaging behavior. Own your story and embrace how your challenges are uniquely preparing you for the contributions you will make. Not everyone will fully understand your experience. Your journey has been custom-designed to grow you specifically for what you are meant to do. The hardships of your story, both big and small, can ignite you to the greatest potential of who you can become. Cooperate with the story that is unfolding, then write a new, more compelling story for your future.

EXERCISES TO DEVELOP A VICTOR MINDSET

1. Lean into the Pain, Follow the Fear

Pay attention to your emotions and feelings as they arise. You don't have to deny them and you don't have to be dominated by them. Be aware and learning. As you notice your emotions, what are the ways you numb out and comfort the pain?

Instead of numbing out, sit with the emotions and process them through your identity-first filter. What are you really afraid of?

Now that you understand how shame is standing in the path of your growth, what is the next vulnerable step you can take that you have been avoiding?

2. Study Your Story

Like you're re-watching game film, review the most painful experiences in your life or the experiences that seem to repeat themselves. Replay them in slow motion, deconstructing how they might be connected to your core fear. You can also think of your favorite songs, your favorite movies, or important decisions you made. Your brain has subconsciously weaved your life around your core fear. Understanding how fear has directed your past can help you subvert its control on your future.

MINDSET 4

VISIONARY MINDSET

———

The ability to see a more advanced version of yourself. Discovering true desire and creating a vision of the future that entices motivation and produces energy in the present moment.

On December 30, 2009, J.D. Collins stood at half court, knowing this would be the last game of his career. Just two possessions into the game his right knee swelled up to the size of a pumpkin, the same knee he injured two weeks prior. Raised on a farm in rural Indiana, J.D. had too much toughness and pride to bow out of the rest of the game, so he managed his way to the final buzzer by taking just two steps to either side of half court. Towards the end of the game, he hobbled over to Michigan State Head Coach Tom Izzo to apologize for his subpar effort. To J.D.'s credit, Izzo wasn't aware of any drop off in his game. What started as a dream of being in an Indiana State High School championship game took him to the NCAA Final Four, but now, at just 47 years old, J.D. knew he would never officiate a college basketball game again.

Before donning a whistle full-time, J.D. spent 10 years as the CEO of a manufacturing company. While climbing the ladder from manager to CEO and part-owner, he spent nights and weekends as a referee on the high school basketball circuit. He was on a mission to officiate a state championship game. However, based on the state's athletic association rules, it would take 10 years of working high school games before he was eligible. That timeline was too slow for his ambition. So, in 1987 he made the jump to college basketball. After just three seasons, he set his sights on the Final Four.

That climb wasn't easy. It started with long, late-night drives across state lines to small colleges throughout the Midwest. It involved navigating politics and relationships across multiple divisions of college basketball. It required ingenuity like befriending a small-plane pilot to expand his reach of potential games. It caused family stress and forced sacrifices. Of all the challenges in reaching the pinnacle, the angry coaches were the easy part.

In 2004 he was selected to his first Final Four as an alternate. For most people, it would have been an ideal position. He received the same paycheck, the same perks, no pressure or scrutiny, and a courtside seat. For J.D., he couldn't help but think, "I should be on that floor." With the seed of desire planted, he set out to become the best referee in college basketball. The plan included working every high-pressure game in America to prepare himself for the big stage, getting in peak physical conditioning, learning the rule book better than he knew his Bible, and improving his communication skills and decision making.

Having a Visionary Mindset is about seeing yourself more advanced than you are right now. Not just in accolades, but in skills, abilities, and character traits. It's about discovering true desire and creating a future vision that entices motivation and produces energy in the present moment. It's more than the goals you set. It's about the person you want to become.

GOALS AREN'T THE SECRET

Before the start of my freshman season of college basketball, Coach Patterson made our entire team gather in the locker room to collaborate on goals for the season. With a marker, poster board, and full confidence, we made our list:

1. Best defensive team in the league.
2. Win 20+ games.
3. Win the conference championship.

It's a familiar list, and for most teams, it would have been acceptable, but our coach challenged us to upgrade our approach. When we set a goal to "make noise at the national tournament," Coach asked us if we intended to take rattles and kazoos to cheer on our conference rival. It stung when he said it, but it wasn't meant to be a snarky belittling of our desires. He was challenging us to be clearer with our vision. And it didn't stop there.

Another goal was to be undefeated at home. Coach asked us, "What happens if we lose our first home game? Do we cancel the rest of them? Is our season over? Should we quit?"

It was then I began to understand that goals are brittle. They can die easily and they are too often impacted by uncontrollable, external variables. What drives you once the goal becomes unreachable? Do you just keep re-writing them until you reach them? How long do you hold onto the goals you aren't reaching? How do you respond when it takes longer than expected? Will you take shortcuts to achieve it quicker?

Goals can help you in the short term. They can give you a checkpoint to track progress, push you across the finish line of a desired project, or become stepping stones in a chosen direction, but they are not the compass. Goals that are not aligned with your true desire can erode you along the process of reaching them. You falsely believe that accomplishing the goal will give you what you are lacking in your mission or community. You believe that it will finally position you to do what you've always wanted and become the type of person everyone respects and accepts. If you pursue a goal only for its outcome, you will pursue it in an unhealthy, inauthentic way. You may even pursue it in a dangerous way that tears others down in the process.

Instead of achievement goals, set being goals. Focus on the development of your character traits and the necessary skills to become the type of person you want to become. Then you will be positioned to do the work you want to do and receive the life you dream of.

If you want to be a starter, you can find a bad enough team to realize your goal. If you want to be a leading scorer, well, every team has one. Instead, focus your attention on becoming the kind of person capable of that responsibility. Develop the necessary skills, grow in your understanding of the team's strategies, and upgrade your capacity to carry the load.

If you want to be a head coach, it's not hard to gather a group and coach them. If you want to ascend to the top leadership position in a particular league, you could brown-nose or back-stab your way to the title. Instead, pursue the qualities of a head coach. What tactical skills do you need to sharpen? What soft skills do you need to learn? What kind of leadership skills do you need to develop? What are the character traits of an effective head coach?

J.D. identified the qualities that would make him an elite referee worthy of the Final Four stage: the ability to perform under pressure, peak physical conditioning, detailed knowledge of the rulebook, and excellent communication and decision-making skills. He set out to grow in those qualities.

> **FOCUS ON WHO YOU WANT TO BECOME MORE THAN WHAT YOU WANT TO ACHIEVE.**

As he was struggling through the climb, he questioned the pursuit: "What if I do all these things and I'm still not good enough to work a Final Four?"

The answer was the process still made him a better version of himself. He would become a better CEO, a better husband, a better community member with these attributes, and that was enough to motivate him to pursue it with all of his ambition.

You don't have to completely trash your goals, although adjusting them may be appropriate. Goals can be helpful, but aligning your purpose with who you want to become creates powerful motivation.

FINDING MOTIVATION

When you think of motivation you probably think of the guest speakers who stand in front of the team yelling to hype you into a particular emotional state. You might think of a coach giving a passionate pre-game speech. I think of ex-NFL linebacker Ray Lewis, painted in elaborate eye black, screaming in my face as I army crawl through a mud pit.

If you think of motivation this way, you notice the fruit of a motivated person. You see their external display of energy. You can't motivate yourself or others on hype alone. If you try to will yourself into a new reality, you may find short-term success, but eventually, you'll wear out and revert to your normal. Sustained energy and true motivation are cultivated out of a vision that is deeper than just conquering an opponent. At the root of this motivation is vision.

If you are feeling frustration within your motivation, you may be stubbornly forcing a way that isn't working. Perhaps what has brought you to this point can't get you past this point. Maybe circumstances have changed and your old motivation doesn't work anymore. Any situation that challenges your motivation is an opportunity to upgrade your mindset. Maybe you experience a career-ending injury. Who will you become next? Maybe you're demoted to an alternate role. How can you remain a valuable contributor? Maybe you lose an inspirational family member. Where can you tap into an even deeper inspiration?

J.D. had to wait 70 days for his knee surgery. He considered it 70 days of grieving what was lost and accepting a new reality. If his identity was built around being an official, he wouldn't have been able to let go. Other referees with similar injuries returned to the court, putting their long-term physical health at risk. J.D. reflected on who he had become in the process of his climb and said, "What's next?" He set a vision to become the national coordinator of officials for the NCAA. Just like preparing to be a Final Four referee, he identified who he would have to become to hold such a position. He became commissioner of a small-college conference in Indiana. The skills he developed in managing league-wide initiatives and working with college presidents prepared him for his next step.

To be an enduring performer, you will have to continually find new motivation to propel yourself forward. No motivation lasts forever. The most powerful motivation comes from a vision that is painted with the colors of your true desires.

SHED THE SHOULDS

I am a cautious driver. I have the mindset that everyone on the road is out to kill me. Maybe they aren't directly aiming for me, but my safety isn't at the forefront of their mind. They are far more interested in that missed text message, their eyeliner, or the double cheeseburger oozing mayonnaise on their khakis. It terrifies me to think these people are operating machinery moving at 55 miles per hour.

My wife, on the other hand, is a citizen's version of Danica Patrick. Driving to the grocery store is a race against unsuspecting competitors. That car in front of her is a loser to overtake. If you ain't first, you're last.

When I'm driving with her in the passenger seat, she doesn't have to say a word. I feel the pressure coming across the center console. I have to drive faster. I feel guilty for driving the speed limit. When I brake at a yellow light I feel like I should apologize. I imagine a scenario when I get pulled over for weaving in and out of traffic and try to explain to the cop how I succumbed to silent pressure. I don't think he would understand.

But you understand because you have felt these pressures too. Maybe not while you're driving, but in your work and relational pursuits. Along the way, unseen pressures are stirring up false motivation and vision. They're causing you to drive faster, pretend to be someone you're not, or take routes not in line with your true desires. Naming those pressures and deconstructing them is the pathway to uncovering your true desires.

There are two prevalent silent pressures influencing people everywhere. The first is the pressure of tradition. The pressure of tradition highlights how it's always been done and makes you believe you have to follow the same path. There are institutions in place that you have to navigate to reach the pinnacle. There is the proverbial ladder you have to climb and the rungs are already set in place. You may find yourself motivated by these predefined stepping stones as the only path to what you want in life. You feel the pressure of conforming to tradition.

The second pressure is the pressure of others. There is an influential person in your life you are trying to please or appease. It could be a parent, a mentor, or a coach. Maybe they haven't explicitly expressed standards or expectations for your climb, but they are implied. Maybe you created them out of your insecurity. The goals you set and the achievements you strive for are an effort to feel close to that person. They might even be out of a desire to actively reject that person, the tradition, or the pressure to conform. Either way, the pressure is clouding your true desire.

To notice these pressures, notice the "shoulds". What do you hear yourself saying you should do or should become? Where should you go? What role should you be in? What do other people say you should have accomplished? These "shoulds" are coming from the voice of shame. You succumb to these pressures to comfort your identity in the face of fear. To shed the pressures, shed the shoulds.

To find your true motivation, surface your true desires. Find a space mentally where there is no judgment and no pretending. Strip away all of the baggage that holds you back from expressing what you truly want. Let your desires rage. Write them down or yell them out. Either way, become unhinged. You may surface desires that are destructive or unhealthy. You may speak desires that seem self-serving. There may be desires that surprise you. You're not broken or ugly for wanting these. You're just ready to move past the pressures of tradition and others that have snuffed out your light until now.

As these desires surface, connect them back to different parts of your story. Are they related to your identity fear discussed with the Relaxed Mindset? Are they related to pressures you are experiencing from tradition and others? Answers to these questions will reveal your motives. You may discover you have been chasing someone else's dream and not your own. You may change your pursuit because of what you learn. It's also possible you maintain the same pursuit with a healthier motivation than just trying to live up to outside pressure.

Ultimately, you will be driven by your desires. Intrinsic motivation is more powerful than extrinsic motivation. If you can't move past the pressure of tradition and others, then you will unknowingly work against your true desires and continually experience restlessness and frustration. Even if you achieve everything you seek, you will be unfulfilled. If you can be honest about what you want, then your forward movement will become true to who you are and you will have no regrets. You will live with an insatiable passion that others will want to be a part of. Your north star is already in you. You need to discover it and accentuate it.

> INTRINSIC MOTIVATION IS MORE POWERFUL THAN EXTRINSIC MOTIVATION. TO FIND YOUR TRUE MOTIVATION, SURFACE YOUR TRUE DESIRES.

YOUR RETIREMENT PARTY

The energy you need to move forward day after day comes from a clear vision that is aligned with your secure identity. The vision motivates you to move forward. In the Victor Mindset, you learned about your past and what experiences have motivated you to this point. Now, look forward to a vision of who you want to become. Write the ending of your story and let that shape your actions and decisions in the present.

Imagine your retirement party. Hundreds of people who you have interacted with are in attendance, from family to friends, teammates to coaches, even fans and boosters. Every retirement party includes speeches from these groups of people about the retiree. They begin with the long list of accomplishments and then always say the required line: "But more than that, he/she was a great person."

Imagine three different people, each representing a different group, giving a speech about you. How do they describe you after the required line? Get past the accomplishments. What do they say about your character? Choose one adjective each group uses to describe you. How do you want to be remembered?

As a coach, I want my players to say I was patient, my family to say I was present, and my colleagues to say I was selfless. For J.D., he wants people to remember that he cared, he was faithful, and he was a man of his word.

These adjectives will become the guiding principles in your life. They will determine how you engage with your community, what job you will take next, and how you interact with difficult teammates or athletes.

Having a Visionary Mindset is about imagining progress, the future, and growth. It's not just imagining what you want to happen in your mission or community. It's imagining the changing of your character. You may want to be Lebron James, but what is it that you truly want in being Lebron? The safety of the money? The status of the celebrity? The accolades? The Visionary Mindset is about imagining a future where those luxuries are already present. You already have the safety, worth, and validation you need. What motivates you then?

You will gravitate towards what you're most compelled by. Imagine your future character potential and then the mission and community that would be built from that. Write a compelling story that stirs up an enduring motivation. Let that pierce through the cloud of pressures and then build your focus around that vision.

EXERCISES TO DEVELOP A VISIONARY MINDSET

1. Surface Your True Desires

Evaluate your goals. Are they achievement goals or are they being goals? What is your motive behind those goals? Is there something you are hoping to get to feel whole? Is there a void in your worth, love, or belonging that you are hoping it will fill? Surface your desires. Write them down or yell them out. Get unhinged. Let them rage. Don't judge yourself. Be honest with yourself so you can grow. Motives reveal the real you.

I desire to accomplish _____

I desire to be known for _____

I desire to have _____

2. Shed the Shoulds

There are unseen pressures impacting your performance and decisions, the pressure of tradition and the pressure of others. Name the pressures and shed the shoulds.

What is the voice of tradition telling you that you "should" do?

Who is the "other" in your life? Even if they aren't influencing you, awareness of the potential threat can be a helpful safeguard.

3. Write A New Ending

Imagine your retirement ceremony. What three groups of people are represented as speakers? It could be family, teammates, friends, fans, or a reporter. What adjective do you want each of them to use to describe you? Display these attributes where you will see them regularly. Let them guide your decision-making and actions each day.

	GROUP	ADJECTIVE
1.		
2.		
3.		
4.		
5.		

MINDSET 5

FOCUSED MINDSET

—

The ability to remove distractions and quiet your mind in the midst of chaos to fully engage the present moment.

So far, you have primarily looked inward and to your past to understand who you are and what impedes your ability to navigate pressure and obstacles. For many, the introspection is difficult. Like rebuilding a muscle that atrophies without use, building habits of introspection will be painful if you don't regularly practice it. The more you practice, the more you will learn to harness the stories, fears, and desires you surface for your advantage. The dark parts of your past that you have been avoiding will become the strengths you capitalize on for your greatest victories.

All the work you have done to this point has laid the foundation for what is to come. If you are distracted internally you won't be able to focus externally. You will blow with the wind, driven by fear and changing every moment. Understanding your identity, becoming aware of fear, surfacing your true desires, and tearing down pressure's pedestals cleared the way of internal distraction. With a vision of your potential fueling motivation, it's time to learn to focus your mind on the present.

This isn't a smoothly paved pathway. Culture is distracting and can cause you to deviate from your true pursuit. People, businesses, and entertainment all try to pull you in different directions. The people you encounter who distract you may be insecure, trying to use you to quiet their own fear. This is the teammate who wants you to affirm their victimhood or the coach who wants you to perform well for the sake of their record. Businesses and entertainment distract you by offering an escape from the pain you feel. However, they only stir up discontent and sell you a solution that falls short of the needs of your identity. It's unrealistic to think you can create an insulated bubble of attention where you're never knocked off balance. Elite performers develop a mindset that recognizes these distractions and refocuses on demand.

Having a Focused Mindset does not mean you have a rigid expression of self-discipline. It's not a furrowed eyebrow or crinkled forehead. It's the ability to find clarity in the heat of the battle. It's the ability to quiet your mind in the craziness of circumstances. It's a relaxed focus; a focus of wonder and awe, when the moment in front of you has your full attention. It is an undistracted presence. You work hard and push yourself, not because you have to or because external forces are driving you, but because you want to. When there is alignment within your life, your pursuit will be an overflow of desire and it will create a laser-like focus.

ELITE PERFORMERS FIND CLARITY IN THE HEAT OF BATTLE AND REFOCUS ON DEMAND.

DISTRACTED BY COMPARISON

When you are driven by shame and the pressure of others, you will be distracted by comparison. Comparison has one benefit and many costs. The example of others can show you possibilities you didn't see before, but comparing your story to their story or your position to their position can derail you. It leaves you chasing fantasies. Instead, allow your view of others to inspire you to hone your abilities. The goal is to become the best version of yourself, not to conquer others.

Throughout my college basketball career, I dominated preseason conditioning. Heading into my senior year, I had a three-year undefeated record for individual races on the track. That summer we recruited a freshman guard who was a high school state champion in cross country. The entire team predicted the end of my reign. I wasn't sure if I could keep up either, but I trained to. On the day of our mile run, I had a strategy in place.

After the first straightaway, when everyone's ego subsided, we settled into our strides. I let him set the pace. I positioned myself one step behind, determined to hold this distance for the duration of the race.

By the third lap, I had fallen behind two more steps. He was shaking out his hands and arms as if playing with a puppy on a jog through the park. I was gasping for energy, wondering if I could sustain for another lap. I had a trump card in my hand but needed to stay close enough to use it.

After the final turn of the third lap, I noticed a green line marking the start of the final straightaway. If I could remain in striking distance during the final lap, the plan was to turn the mile run into a 100-yard sprint as soon as we crossed that green line.

By lap four I grit my teeth. It was no longer a battle of conditioning. It became a battle of will and determination. When I hit that green line, four steps behind, I kicked in the afterburners. The only fuel left in the tank was a lifetime of bragging rights.

It was enough.

I crossed the finish line one second ahead of the long-distance champ. Record intact.

The beauty of this story is not in the conquering of an opponent. The real success is that I ran the fastest mile of my life.

4:55.

Never before. Never again.

Competition pushed me to perform my best. Not comparison.

Comparison is thinking you need to run the race exactly like others do. Competition is running your best race vs. their best race.

Comparison is trying to always stay one step ahead of your competitors.

Competition is creating a strategy that you can win.

Comparison is training the same way others do.

Competition is finding your optimal training practices to push yourself past previous limits.

Comparison distracts. Competition drives focus.

Comparison shames. Competition sharpens.

Only one wins in comparison. Both can win in competition.

BE YOUR OWN BEST COACH

Competition can bring out the best in people. It can also reveal the worst. Ambitious athletes tend to be their own biggest critic. I have worked with professional athletes who berate themselves with name-calling and cuss words after every missed shot or mistake. There is no grace for imperfection. It's promoted as virtuous, ignoring the damage it does to your identity.

For most athletes, their self-talk has been programmed by the lie they believe about who they are. "You're no good. If you don't make enough shots your career may be over. If you stop now, Dad won't drive you to any more hockey games." For others, their self-talk is modeled after influential coaches. Many athletes gravitate towards coaches who match the voice of their shame. They believe they are bad, so they seek out the coach who reinforces this narrative. They believe no amount of success is enough, so they don't accept praise and subject themselves to coaches who constantly criticize.

If you're noticing this is true about your situation, don't beat yourself up. Developing your awareness of shame and fear helps you decipher between the insecure coaches and the healthy voices that take you the farthest, fastest. Not everyone is in a position to choose their coach. You may have to make the best of your circumstances. Start by becoming your own best coach.

THE GOAL IS TO BECOME THE BEST VERSION OF YOURSELF, NOT TO CONQUER OTHERS.

Recall the core fear you related to in the Relaxed Mindset. Underneath each fear is a desire you long for at your core. When you discover that desire, you can reprogram your self-talk with an affirmation statement to give yourself exactly what you need when you need it most.

If you fear not being needed, the desire you are searching for is love. You need to know that you can still be a playmaker even if you're not the primary playmaker. Regardless if everything depends on you, your gifts are important to the success of the team. When you feel an abundance of love, winning will become more important to you than individual stats.

If you fear not being taken care of, the desire you need fulfilled is joy. You won't find that joy from working harder or more often. True joy comes from creativity and unique problem-solving. What was it like when you first started playing, when you first fell in love with the sport? Recapture the wonder of your inner child to express the joy you have been lacking.

If you are afraid you don't belong, you are craving peace. Peace doesn't come from the absence of problems or deficiencies. There will always be problems and you will always have areas you can improve. If you change teams, your weaknesses will follow you. You need to feel like a welcomed member of the team, with all of your strengths, weaknesses, and quirks accepted. Then you work to improve your game because you are a valued member of the team, not to become a valued member of the team.

If you feel inadequate, you need to give yourself patience. No one will give you the patience you need to make the next jump in your development. Growth comes out of struggle. Mastery comes by doing. Be patient with yourself in the process. Competition is more about learning and growing than achieving.

If you fear that you can't perform well enough to feel worthy, you need the gift of kindness. You don't have to earn your worth. No amount of success will make you feel satisfied. Be kind to yourself. Measure your success by how much fun you have while you play.

If you fear that you are a bad person, you need the gift of goodness. The negative results that happen in your life are not a reflection of who you are as a person. You are good at your core. Negative outcomes don't define you. They are clues to where you can grow.

If you fear that if you mess up the worst will happen, you need to feel the security of faithfulness. It's not a guarantee that it will all work out exactly as you want it to, but it is a guarantee that who you are will remain intact in the process. You will make mistakes, but that is the process of growing. The more you push yourself to the edge of your abilities and commit to a decision, the more you will learn what works and doesn't work. Don't wait for certainty. The time to act is now.

If you fear being vulnerable, learn the gift of gentleness. You don't have to match strength for strength. You don't have to come out on top of every conflict. Your expressions of vulnerability can be a strength to win in the long run. It can build a stronger team and attract more followers. The more you learn to be gentle with yourself in vulnerable situations, the more you will recognize the fear of others as well. They are proving and hiding just like you are.

If you fear you are not seen for your uniqueness, you need the gift of self-control. You don't have to test life to see if anyone notices. You don't have to sit quietly and wait to be called on. You can own the spotlight when your strengths are needed and you can share the spotlight to highlight a teammate. You don't have to destructively over-indulge in secret while publicly portraying a life of discipline, and you don't have to force your rigid ways on others. Your self-discipline is a strength. It can also be a weakness.

Rewriting your self-talk is not just about thinking positive. It's not hype. It's about meeting the needs of your identity and it is most powerful when leveraged with your imagination.

RE-WIRE THE BRAIN

We explored in previous chapters how past experiences have shaped you and your present responses. They didn't just shape you. They shaped your brain too. Your brain wired around each experience, constructing a defense mechanism to protect you from false threats to your identity. It has been conditioned to respond that way ever since. You can't undo those wirings, but you can re-wire the brain with a new baseline.

Imagine you are a rookie about to take the court for your first career game. The entire team huddles in the locker room for one last pep talk. You are selected to lead the team onto the court. With all of your

> **REPROGRAM YOUR SELF-TALK WITH AN AFFIRMATION STATEMENT TO GIVE YOURSELF WHAT YOU NEED.**

youthful exuberance, you run out of the tunnel, waving your arms to excite the crowd. When you reach center court, you look back to find out no one else ran with you. All of your teammates are standing in the tunnel, laughing and pointing. You just fell for the oldest prank in the book. You laugh it off to protect your ego, but the damage has been done.

This powerful experience caused your brain to wire a lie about your belonging. It will try to protect you from any future pain. From now on, whenever you take the court, you will look over your shoulder or hide in the back of the line to make sure you are not left alone. You will take the court with a little less enthusiasm. Shame has stolen a piece of your identity and increased the stress in your mind.

You perform your best with a still mind, not an anxious or overactive one. The elite performers can achieve a calm state of focus on demand. This is where mindfulness helps but doesn't go far enough. The brain is shaped by experiences. To override the wirings of shame, you have to give it a more powerful experience.

GIVE YOURSELF WHAT YOU NEED

Three components shape your awareness of who you are: your psychology, how you process what's happening; your neurology, the wiring of your brain; and your physiology, your body. You have learned about the superior psychology of processing your life through identity first. Now, you will learn how to physiologically position your body to rewire the neurology of your brain so that you feel secure in the present moment.

During my first year as an assistant coach in the NBA G League, I worked for a head coach who was intentional about developing his staff. I was preparing to be a head coach, so he allowed me to experience it first-hand during the first half of our final game of the season. He sat on the bench and made suggestions as any assistant would. I was responsible for play calling, timeouts, and making substitutions.

We told the team about the arrangement during our pre-game meeting, but no one else was aware of it. Coincidentally, my parents were in the stands along with a half dozen coaching friends. As players were making their final preparations to take the court, I overheard them snickering about the plan amongst themselves. It stirred an uneasiness in my gut. I began to feel a tightness in my stomach. I noticed my voice start to quiver. I felt a desire to call it off and go back to my position as an assistant coach. It wasn't for lack of confidence or preparedness. I had been preparing for this for years. It was the fear I felt in my identity. It was the crippling voice of shame telling me I wasn't unique enough for this special opportunity. It was telling me to retreat to my place as an assistant and to fit in with the rest of the group. I felt the urge to hide from my spotlight moment. Instead, I leaned into the fear.

Before we took the court, I found a quiet corner of the arena. I closed my eyes and took a deep breath. I escaped to a place called "identity space" and gave myself exactly what I needed.

In my identity space, I imagined a special announcement to all the fans about my promotion. I heard the broadcasters highlighting it over the telecast. I imagined a standing ovation of support. I imagined taking the court with the rest of the staff, the players, and even the fans behind me. They were all running with me and rooting for my success.

What I received in my identity space was permission to own the spotlight. Not in a way that made me the center of attention, but in a way that made me feel secure enough to lead our team with authentic, undistracted presence.

To develop a Resilient Mindset, you used your imagination to detach your identity from the results. The identity space uses your imagination to experience the security of who you are so you can focus and engage without inhibition. It is a place in your mind's eye where you feel whole, where you feel no shame, and where you can feel delight in simply being you. You can embrace all of your uniqueness, struggles, and uncertainties. You can receive new insight or a revelation about the next step.

The place you imagine can be real, fantasy, a place you have been, or a place you would like to go to. My particular spot that night was a favorite waterfall hike along a creek in Arizona. Yours might be a beach, a quiet spot in the woods, or a family member's house that you associate with feeling at peace.

You don't have to pressure yourself into finding the perfect place. Just be wherever comes to mind. Let scenes pass through your awareness and settle in wherever you feel safe. This place can change over time or you may utilize the same place for years. If you're feeling stuck, think of where you would go if you had no responsibilities and acquired an unexpected amount of time, energy, and money.

Close your eyes and go there. Turn up the senses. What do you see? What do you hear? What do you feel? Make it as vivid as possible. Increase the detail. Turn up the volume of a particular sound. Reach out and touch the textures. You can view this space in first person, third person, or switch back and forth. Time doesn't exist. Activities that normally take hours can happen in seconds. Run, jump, swim, or sink into the sand.

Feeling the wholeness of who you are outside of obligations and expectations will help still your mind in anxious situations. You can take it a step further by giving yourself what you need. Remember, experiences shape the brain, not lessons, speeches, or knowledge. Turn your affirmation statement into an experience. Inside your identity space, imagine writing a message in the ground and make it a part of you. Or, like I did, see the support of your community regardless of the results. The laws of physics don't apply. Let your subconscious lead. Surrender to the experience.

> YOU CAN'T STRESS YOURSELF INTO A FOCUSED MINDSET. IT STARTS INTERNALLY WITH A RELAXED PRESENCE.

You can't stress yourself into a Focused Mindset. It can't be achieved by increasing your intensity. It starts internally with a relaxed presence, which produces clarity.

Use your identity space as a daily practice to build a new baseline. When you know what center feels like you will notice when you are knocked off-center, even in the smallest moments. You can also use your identity space to prepare for a stressful experience like when I prepared to coach the game. As you practice more and more, you will learn to drop into this space in the middle of a stressful experience, remove the distraction of shame, and recover on the fly. It doesn't stop at just sitting still. Following the internal work of the Focused Mindset, you will move to external action. The inspiration has to go somewhere. The Process Mindset will activate it.

I would love to tell you that we won the game because of my brilliant coaching. We didn't. There are no guarantees in mission and community. But you can guarantee that you will show up to every moment, fully present, fully engaged, ready to enjoy and capitalize on what it has to offer.

EXERCISES TO DEVELOP A FOCUSED MINDSET

1. Write Your Affirmation Statement
Pay attention to your self-talk. Is it coming from the voice of shame? Be your own best coach by learning to give yourself what you need. If you haven't identified your core fear yet, this may be another angle to reveal what it is you feel you are lacking most in your identity. Write an affirmation statement that calms your fear.

2. Build Your Identity Space
Create your identity space in your mind's eye. Close your eyes. Settle into your seat. Feel the weight of your body. Take a couple deep belly breaths. Let your subconscious lead your mind to a place that you feel safe and taken care of. It could be a place you have been before, somewhere you would like to go, or someplace completely made up. Turn up all of the senses. What do you see? What do you hear? What do you feel? Reach out and touch something. With your eyes closed, imagine writing a word or phrase to yourself. Then make this a part of you. See it penetrate your physical body. Remember, the laws of physics don't apply here. Before you leave this space, go play. Do an activity, explore, or take an adventure. There is no shame here, no obligations, no responsibilities. Feel what it's like to delight in being you.

MINDSET 6

PROCESS MINDSET

——

Loving the process of skill building. Utilizing routines and triggers to stay prepared and position yourself for peak experiences on demand.

Think about a great performance you witnessed. A heroic moment in a great time of need. What was the outcome? The moment doesn't stand out to you because of an incredible blunder. It stands out because it produced results. Performance matters. Scores are real, but the score isn't the foundation. The great performances you marvel at are built upon thousands of hours of practice and skill-building. Clutch performances aren't a fluke. They occur when preparation meets opportunity. Those opportunities usually come when the stakes are highest and are often unplanned, making it more difficult to access the work of your preparation. Processes, routines, and triggers can help you access the skills you have worked so hard to develop when you need them most.

You already live a life full of processes, some positive and some negative. When you receive feedback from a coach or boss and shut down or respond defensively, that's a process. When you catch a bad break and it knocks you off balance for a week, that's a process. When the opportunity you've been asking for finally arrives and you repeat the same self-sabotaging mistakes, that's a process. Filtering your experiences through the lens of identity first is a superior process to produce elite performance.

With a Process Mindset, you build routines and triggers to enhance what you gained in the Focused Mindset. After doing the internal work to sharpen your focus, build a system that helps you maintain momentum, recapture it when it's lost, or stay alert and ready for when your moment arrives. Routines and triggers prepare your mind. Falling in love with practice prepares your skills.

LOVE THE PRACTICE

You're probably familiar with the tale of David and Goliath. The diminutive citizen slays the mighty warrior with merely a slingshot. It's a classic story that has inspired underdog triumphs for centuries. Have you ever wondered what happened leading up to that moment? Who is David and how did he become the person capable of toppling the giant? Where did he get the courage? Where did he learn the skills? More than the story of triumph, I am inspired by the preparation it took to become the champion. What did David do to prepare for that moment?

David was a shepherd and the youngest of eight brothers. While his older brothers were soldiers who followed the king into battle, David was relegated to the fields to tend to his father's sheep. He was responsible for guiding the sheep to green pastures and calm waters. He was also responsible for protecting them against predators such as lions and wolves. His defense weapon was a slingshot. See where I'm headed with this?

Life as a shepherd is probably boring. Sheep aren't the most exciting creatures. If he did his job well, not every day in those fields was an adventure with lions and wolves on the attack. It seems to me that he had plenty of time to practice a lot of things like public speaking or how he planned to pop the question. Although he was probably more pragmatic, creating challenges to practice his slingshot skills. I envision David setting up Coke cans and knocking them down from varying distances. Maybe as he gained confidence, he balanced a can on a sheep's head to test his accuracy.

Life as a shepherd is also probably lonely. David spent hours and days out in the fields, away from civilization with a flock of friends who don't speak. There was plenty of time for reflection. I imagine there were times he questioned the direction of his life. He probably experienced desires to be in the front line of the battlefield with his brothers. He probably second-guessed the king's decisions, dreaming of the day when he would rule.

David could have pouted in the weeds about his low status as a shepherd. He could have been jealous of his brothers' seemingly higher status. He could have eroded in comparison. He could have been completely unprepared to seize his moment when it arrived.

More likely, David probably showed up, every day, and became a master at his craft. He probably stayed disciplined to a routine, never missing a day to take the sheep out. He was probably focused on becoming the best shepherd in the tribe, all the while falling in love with the process of sharpening his skills. He probably invested himself when no one was watching and when there was no immediate payoff for his work. He probably prepared himself for a championship moment by excelling in the mundane.

After all, there is no healthy overnight success. The line between practice and payoff isn't short. David didn't just march into the valley and slay the giant with one lucky shot. He was a skilled craftsman who used his time in the fields to develop elite skills. He made the mundane monumental by choosing the process of a master. When his opportunity came, he was prepared.

When you feel like you're being overlooked, when you catch yourself gawking at other people climbing the ladder, when you start comparing titles, or when you feel like you're falling behind, redirect your attention to developing your skills. When you're convinced it's your time, but the opportunity isn't there yet, keep slinging your stone. Maybe you can knock down the Coke can, but can you do it 10 times in a row? Can you do it with one eye closed? Can you do it with your weak hand? Keep enhancing your precision. You will need it when the opportunity comes knocking. You get to choose what you want to be great at. Make an authentic choice to be great at the skills that are an overflow of the purpose and the impact you want to have on the world, and then set yourself on a course to mastery.

VALUE OF THE ROUTINE

Elite preparation is built on a routine. The highest performing people live by a systemized routine. It looks different for everyone depending on preferences and personalities, but they all have one. The routine keeps you prepared. It's the consistency you can lean on when you're struggling to find hope and encouragement. Most of life's greatest opportunities come unannounced. It's a terrible feeling to not be ready because you were sulking about not getting a chance.

You probably already live by routines. You have a morning routine or an evening routine. Pay attention next time you get in your car. You have a certain order you put the key in, start the ignition, buckle your seatbelt, choose the music, and put the car in gear. You probably also have performance routines. A pregame routine you follow or an order in which you put on your uniform and lace up your shoes. Michael Jordan always laced up his own shoes. If anyone else laced them up, he threw the shoes out and started over with a new pair.

All of your routines are valuable and important in their own way. Most of them, though, have probably been created unconsciously. You don't even realize you are doing them. My dog knows my routines better than I do. When I get home and change into my hiking shoes, he runs to his water bowl to hydrate, knowing we are about to go on a walk. At 8:30 each night he sits by the patio swing, waiting on permission for cuddle time. He knows it's coming. If you become consciously aware of the routines you are using, you can strategically build them to prepare you to be at your best.

As you build your routine, think about the qualities and skills of who you want to become that you identified with the Visionary Mindset. If you have a vision of being able to do 10 pushups when you reach age 75, then incorporate pushups into your routine. If you want your family to know you care about them, find a way to show that as part of your routine. If you want to consistently live from a secure identity, then perhaps your routine should include time in your identity space. Evaluate the routines you are using. Are they preparing you to become the athlete, coach, or person you desire to be?

You won't always have exceptional motivation. You will have to endure seasons of loneliness and despair. When you don't feel like doing what you need to do, fall back on the routine to continue developing in the direction you desire to go. As artist Mumford and Sons sang, you can "hold on to what you believe in the light, when the darkness has robbed you of all your sight."

> **HOLD ON TO WHAT YOU BELIEVE IN THE LIGHT, WHEN THE DARKNESS HAS ROBBED YOU OF ALL YOUR SIGHT.**
> **MUMFORD & SONS**

BUILD TRIGGERS

For an extra layer of fun and impact, consider building triggers into your routines. You learned earlier how negative triggers have been unintentionally wired into your psyche through pain, shame, and fear. You can also intentionally build triggers to use for your advantage.

During my first year in professional sports, I trained myself to fall asleep on the plane whenever we traveled. 30,000 feet in the air with no cell service was the perfect chance to unplug and catch up on lost sleep. An entire season of this habit built a trigger. Now, any time I go to an airport I immediately become sleepy. No matter the time of day or how many hours I slept the night before, I'm a walking zombie passing through the security line.

One offseason I experimented with creating a trigger I could use during the grueling parts of the basketball season. Every evening that summer I went to the pool with a smoothie. No cell phone, no work, no distractions. I just enjoyed the relaxation. I mindfully sipped my smoothie, feeling the cool temperature on my lips, the texture of the ingredients, and the taste of the fruit. I closed my eyes and soaked up the warmth of the sun. When I finished my drink, I jumped in the pool. I didn't just dip my toe in to check the temperature. I went for it. Full submersion, a shock to the system, allowing the sudden change of temperature to invigorate me. I kept this same routine consistently throughout the offseason. By the time the season arrived, I had successfully built a trigger around this experience. During all of our travel and winter's gloom, whenever I felt frustrated, stuck, or just needed a boost, I drank a smoothie. It immediately triggered my mind state back to being at the pool where I felt completely relaxed and taken care of.

Triggers aren't meant to be a bridge to escape what is happening in front of you. It's about calming your mind so you can think clearly, perform freely, and accelerate your growth. Before diving into the work of building your triggers, try to recognize the ones that already exist in your life. There are songs that take you back to your childhood, smells that remind you of grandma's house, or foods that you eat before every race. There may be negative triggers that aren't serving you well. They take you to hurtful experiences in your past or put you in a more anxious state. You can help yourself by deconstructing and eliminating those.

The most effective triggers are built around the feelings you have. They trick the brain into a particular state of mind. Remember, the brain doesn't discern between perception and reality. What it feels is real. This is why I could feel the sensation of sitting by the pool even though I was stuck in Milwaukee, Wisc., in January with computer problems.

Pay attention to when you feel great, when you have a lot of energy, or when you're especially motivated and creative. What happened just before then? Did you hear a particular song? Read an encouraging word? Eat a certain food? Is there an activity that stirs up these emotions that you can build a trigger around? I have built triggers around water skiing, sitting by a campfire, and playing frisbee. Find a physical activity that matches the emotional experience you had in your identity space. Then layer it with sensations. Make it as visceral as possible. Add music, tastes, and textures. Think of all your senses and how you can stimulate them into tricking your brain. Then be consistent with it. The trigger won't be developed in a day or a week. Keep immersing yourself in the experience until it sticks.

The more advanced you become in your trigger-building, the more you can tie them to your performance. Incorporate them into your training sessions so they are prepared to serve you when you need it most. I worked with a basketball player who patted his leg before shooting a free throw. He trained a calm presence around the leg pat in practice. When the pressure increased in the game, his brain didn't recognize the new scenario. It responded to the training of the leg pat. With an advanced trigger, you can be intentional about the music you hear when you walk to the plate for your at-bat in the bottom of the 9th inning of a tie game.

As your triggers and routines solidify, experiment with reducing their parts so you can deploy them on demand. There will be times when you can't go through your whole routine. The bus shows up late. Plans change. Is your trigger so strong that you can hear just one bar of the song and still trigger the state? Do you have a process for re-centering at halftime after a poor first half? Can you recover during the changeover or while walking to the next hole?

Have fun with this. Experiment. Be creative. This is an opportunity to leverage activities you enjoy to anchor the security of your identity and choose the presence you will bring to competition.

MANIFESTING AND ATTUNING

These processes, routines, and triggers are not meant to be a rigid prescription for accomplishing a New Year's Resolution. They're not a punishment to whip yourself into shape. Remember, no lasting behavioral change is made on willpower alone. They're also not a superstition that guarantees your success. It's not the routine or the trigger that makes you a champion. You become a champion because of your ability to step into these mindsets on demand. Don't become too attached to the routines and processes. They exist to serve you. They give you valuable information about what is or isn't working, about when it's time to adjust, or about when you're ready to upgrade.

If you're blowing with the wind, every day is a random, unpredictable event. It becomes difficult to recreate good performances or isolate what caused poor performances.

> **ROUTINES ARE NOT SUPERSTITIONS THAT GUARANTEE SUCCESS. THEY PREPARE YOUR ABILITY TO STEP INTO THESE MINDSETS ON DEMAND.**

Developing a routine keeps you focused on where you are headed and who you want to become. As you manifest this vision, be sure to also attune to reality. Mike Tyson famously declared everyone has a plan until they get hit in the mouth. The enduring athletes and coaches are simultaneously future-focused and present engaged. They are focused on who they want to become and committed to the routine and plan to get them there. They are also aware of shifts in the tides, paying attention to relevant interruptions. Without a plan, you can't recognize the shifts. It is the nimbleness and malleability of an elite mindset. You can cooperate with what is unfolding while bringing your best self regardless of the circumstances.

EXERCISES TO DEVELOP A PROCESS MINDSET

1. Build Your Routine

Evaluate your current routines. What routines do you need to dismantle because they aren't serving you well?

What routines do you need to adjust because they aren't working like they used to?

What new routines can you build that align with the skills you want to develop and the qualities you desire, and that position yourself for the mind state you need?

2. Build Your Trigger

Find a physical activity that brings you the delight and joy you experienced in your identity space and experiment with building a trigger around that activity. Layer it with sensations that can help you tap into the experience on demand. Then practice it consistently for the trigger to have its deepest impact.

What activity will you use (i.e. playing catch with your child)?

What song will you play during the activity?

What will you eat or drink immediately before, during, or immediately after the activity?

What object from the activity will you take to the office or locker room that reminds you of the experience?

EMPATHETIC MINDSET

———

The ability to be the most emotionally aware person on the team; where vulnerability becomes a strength to manage conflict, advance the group, and build a team you enjoy.

For 31 years my dad built a small-college basketball dynasty in mid-Missouri. National tournaments, conference championships, Hall of Fames, name on the court, all of the best stuff successful coaches accomplish. Because he stayed at one school for so long, it became a family affair. I was practically raised in the gym. From early morning conditioning, to after school practice, and late-night games, it was my second home. They say my sister and I took naps in the ball cage as infants.

Because it was my father, and because the wins and losses affected whether we got ice cream or not, I was emotionally invested in the outcome of his games. My friends and I were the water boys and self-designated baseline hecklers. When our rival's All-American center dramatically fell to the floor with a mildly sprained ankle, interrupting the game for far too long, I yelled, "Take him off the court! Let's keep playing!" The 7-footer promptly stood up on two solid feet, flashed me a not-so-nice gesture, and ran off the court.

When I reached high school, I moved to more comfortable seats for the games and my comments became more mature – and bolder. It was Coach Burchard night at the "Cougar Dome" and every fan received a life-sized cutout of my dad's face glued to a stick. It was one of the school's many promotions highlighting my dad's red mustache and habit of chain drinking Diet Coke. As any mischievous child would, I hoarded more than one as keepsakes to be used later. On that particular night, I put them to good use.

In the middle of the first half, my dad took his starting forward out of the game for making a mistake. The player's dad was sitting directly across the court from the bench and voiced his displeasure. It was a small, intimate gym, so anyone paying attention heard his comments. Then the replacement player immediately made his own mistake. The starter's dad questioned the decision: "Why don't you take him out too?"

My dad was fuming at the outburst, but he bit his tongue to keep from shouting a rebuttal. He couldn't say what was on his mind, but I could. I walked over to the parent and handed him my Coach B facemask. "Here, do you want to be Coach Burchard tonight?"

He slapped the face out of my hand and I returned to my seat. It was the closest I've ever been to a real-life my-dad-can-beat-up-your-dad scenario and my dad witnessed the entire exchange.

During the second half, he made me sit next to him on the bench. I was sure I was in big trouble. Nothing ever took his focus off the game. Not even the time my mom made me tell him that his zipper was open. Instead, he gave me a message that altered the trajectory of the rest of my basketball career.

He told me I had a decision to make. I could be an athlete who was serious about becoming a great player, or I could be a fan, heckling from the sidelines. He used that moment to challenge me to upgrade my mindset. (For the record, a couple of days later he did thank me for standing up to the parent.)

When you internalize the six mindsets you have learned so far, you will not only perform at a level above most of your peers, but you will see all of life through an entirely different lens. You will notice when others are stuck and what has them stuck. You will be able to communicate with them in a way that gives them clarity and unblocks their flow. Like the story of every superhero, you will have to decide whether you will use your superpowers for your own gain or you will use them to better the world around you. Like my dad challenged me, you will have to decide to level up your position.

This is the turning point for the elite performers who become champions. You won't realize the full potential of your mission unless you actively build the team that is supporting and improving it. The coach or athlete with average talent who is part of a high-performing team will always go farther than a more talented individual performer that has no support. Even if you compete in an individual sport, you are not on a solo climb. People are investing in your success and others want to. When you intentionally invest in them, you will reap exponential results compared to trying to do it by yourself. To experience the full power of these kinds of relationships, you need empathy.

GIVE WHAT YOU NEED

Empathy is not forced or manufactured. It is a result of a secure identity. When you are no longer obsessed with your status, you will notice others. When you are no longer driven by the desire to be seen, known, and heard, you can make others feel seen, known, and heard. You will have such a deep presence that you can put yourself in their shoes.

Having an Empathetic Mindset does not mean you just comfort their pain and enable a victim mindset. Instead, you transfer the emotion you feel for others into action to help move them forward. When your status increases and displaces a teammate, you find ways to shine the spotlight back on them. You pass the baton to a co-worker with good ideas and valuable skills who is overlooked or undervalued. You create space for the new person to feel like she belongs. This is expressed differently by everyone. When you have a secure identity, you will express the authentic version of yourself. You may be a teddy bear off the field even though you're a bruiser on the field. You may express with a competitive fire that makes others cringe, but your teammates know you care about them.

The easiest way to start building up your team is to give what you need. When you feel the pain of loneliness, find a way to make someone else feel like they belong. When you struggle to be patient with yourself, give someone else patience. I coached a player who was trying hard to be the leader of the team. As a fourth-year veteran, he felt a responsibility to fill the leadership role. At the end of every practice, game, and team meeting he huddled the group for a pep talk. His intentions were good but his voice wasn't heard and it frustrated him. I advised him to give his position away. Instead of being the final voice of every huddle, I told him to empower a teammate to lead the breakout. For the rest of the season, he picked a different teammate to finish each huddle. He picked the person everyone was already following, the shy rookie, and even the teammate he didn't like. The energy of the team changed and he began to smile again.

Shame makes you believe a lie about who you are. Fear makes you express that belief by trying to take what you think you need from others. Throw a counter punch by giving what you need to others, stripping shame of its power.

> WHEN YOU ARE NO LONGER OBSESSED WITH YOUR STATUS, YOU WILL NOTICE OTHERS.

FOR COACHES

As a coach, you have a greater responsibility to understand the fears and desires of each of your athletes. When facing a challenging player, don't just say, "This is who I am and they have to deal with it." That approach fails to recognize your capacity to develop a dynamic leadership voice. "Listen to what I say, not how I say it," is a copout for a mediocre coach. Don't ask your developing athletes to be the mature one in the relationship. Order your internal world so you don't have to ask them to absorb your insecurities.

The insecure coach is attached to a style with no flexibility to adjust. You don't have to be narrowly defined by your coaching style. Coaching and leading are roles you fill. Your style is shaped by your experiences, your desires, and the needs of your athletes. If you base your coaching approach by what you see on TV or perceive in others, you will probably miss the bigger picture. You might see a raging figurehead march up and down the sideline, screaming at every possession. What you may not see are the hugs and relational conversations that happen every day outside the lines.

You have a voice that is unique to you and has been shaped by who you are. When you discover that voice you will have the dynamic range to connect with each player on your team exactly where they are. You will move in and out of styles as necessary. Like Jeff Hornacek from earlier in the book, you will turn up or turn down the volume of intensity as needed. You will also be able to show different parts of your personality when appropriate. When the team needs stability in turbulent waters, you can wear the cape of a leader. When the team needs inspiration, you can wear the hat of a storyteller to spark their motivation. During your preseason bonding activities, you can set your armor down and let loose the playfulness of a child.

In 2009 my dad's team made an improbable run through the national tournament. After starting the conference season 2-3, they won 13 of their next 14 games, including the conference championship on the road. The winning streak continued into the national tournament where they won four games in five days to advance to the championship game for the first time in school history. As the wins accumulated, my dad likened the season to riding a wave in the ocean. He encouraged his players to enjoy it as long as it lasted. The team marshaled their energy around the motto, "Ride the wave." By the third win of the tournament, my dad was surfing on top of tables in the locker room to celebrate. Pictures of him stroking his hair in the breeze went viral. It was a side fans and players rarely saw from the foot-stomping, fiery redhead.

Taking on these different characteristics is not fake or inauthentic. You can still be true to who you are while moving in and out of different roles. When you're secure in who you are, you won't be restrained by an image you feel forced to portray at all times. Instead, you will be fully engaged with the moment, showing up to give exactly what it needs.

FILLING, CREATING, AND MEETING SPACE

There are three specific roles every coach needs to fill depending on the situation: leader, sage, and empath. You can think of these roles as you think of space in sports. Sometimes you take up space to gain an advantage, sometimes you create space to gain an advantage, and sometimes you meet space. Your team is dealing with these same dynamics. As a leader you will fill space, as a sage you will create space, and as an empath you will meet space. It

DON'T DENY YOUR EMOTIONS AND DON'T BE DOMINATED BY THEM. BE AWARE AND LEARN.

may help to understand these roles better in the context of a house party.

A couple times each year the owner of the Phoenix Suns invited the entire team and staff to his house for dinner. "House" doesn't do his mansion justice, and "dinner" doesn't adequately describe the feast. The palace had all of the luxuries – an outdoor living room next to the pool, a full-sized soccer field, a weight room, and the court from the 2009 NBA All-Star game. Not to mention the labyrinth of rooms connected like a maze, and the busy workers hired to clean the house and host the team. There was even a parking attendant just to direct us to the appropriate entrance.

A leader fills space. No rookie player or coach ever wanted to be the first to arrive at the party. The house was so big you were afraid of getting lost. You needed a leader to show up first and fill the space of uncertainty.

When your team is walking into uncharted territory, or when you're in a dark or unsettling phase, they need a leader to guide them through the space. You need to step out in front and show them the way. Model the behavior, comfort their uncertainty, and give clear direction.

A sage creates space. Like any party, there were times when everyone gathered in the same room and it became too crowded. When the party becomes stale and no one is sure where to go next, the team needs a sage. The sage stokes curiosity and interest in new possibilities. When your team is stuck or lacking inspiration, tell stories that guide them to new revelations. Give a glimpse into what they might find in the other room or what might happen if they directed their energy in a new way. Suggest the new reality but let them discover it.

An empath meets space. There is always that one person who runs off to a room all by himself. He removes himself from the group. Maybe there's a strong emotion that pulls him to hide. Maybe it's a protest against what is happening. The empath meets space by assessing the emotional state and meeting them where they are.

When I confronted the fan for criticizing my dad during the game, my dad filled the space between me and the fan by making me sit next to him on the bench during the second half (leader). He then created space in my world by opening my mind to a potential new reality that I was left to discover (sage). Two days later, he addressed the insecurity I was feeling from the encounter by thanking me for being so bold (empath).

You won't naturally excel in all of these roles. You are likely strong in one, weak in another, and mediocre in the other. The point is not to recognize your strength and build your entire approach around that. Your brilliance as a coach is your ability to grow in all three and your awareness of when to use them. Like any skill or mindset that you are developing, it takes practice to master the different roles. There is no perfect. It's like a chef experimenting with an entrée. You don't change the core of who you are, but you sprinkle in different spices and experiment with different combinations to enhance the flavor.

As you try on these different roles and reveal different elements of your personality with your team, pay attention to their feedback. Like a comedian experimenting with jokes, your athletes and teammates will show you what they accept from you by how they respond. It won't be the same for each player or each team and it could change within the same player or team. As you coach them to be aware of space on the court, model the same off the court by filling space, creating space, and meeting space as needed.

VULNERABILITY IS A SUPERPOWER

The key to successfully executing these roles is vulnerability. The insecure performers see vulnerability as a weakness. It can be a weakness if you unload your junk on the team, forcing them to carry the weight of your burdens. However, when it is expressed out of a secure identity, vulnerability is a strength, not a weakness. It becomes the superpower that binds your team. When you can lead the way with vulnerability, it relaxes everyone. They won't feel uptight and tense with the pressure of having to live up to an unrealistic standard. They won't blame others or cover up mistakes for fear of being the weakest link. Your vulnerability will stimulate an environment focused more on growth than perfection.

There are two ways you can start leading with vulnerability. The first is to tear down your pedestals. Your title naturally props you up on a pedestal. Whether it is Coach, Head Coach, Veteran, or Leading Scorer, your title implies superiority. The insecure leader will manipulate situations to hold onto the status. The secure leader will give status away by highlighting the people who help you score, calling yourself out when you try to prove or hide, admitting you don't know the answer, or making someone else the expert. As a head coach, I included my mistakes in video sessions, I apologized for a poor practice plan if they didn't bring enough energy, and I took all of the criticism when I didn't remind them of picture day soon enough to schedule haircut appointments. You can inspire them with your wins, but relax them with your struggles too.

One game we had a reserve player energize a comeback at the beginning of the fourth quarter. With about six minutes remaining in the game, he asked for a sub because he was tired. It's rare for a player to have that kind of selfless approach, so when I took him out I told him, "Catch your breath and I'll put you back in."

Then his replacement played just as well. He not only kept the lead but extended it. I became afraid to change anything and possibly lose momentum, so I never put the original player back in the game. The next day I pulled that player aside and apologized: "I'm sorry I didn't put you back in the game. The team was playing well and I was afraid of making a change. But I respect your selflessness to ask for a sub. Thank you for doing that."

Acknowledging how your decisions might affect the emotional state of your teammates or athletes goes a long way in building trust. Find ways to make them feel seen, known and heard. Instead of trying to be the smartest person in the room, aim to be the most aware.

The second way you can start leading with vulnerability is to ask for what you need. When you notice your insecurity flare up based on a teammate's words or actions, don't fire back with your own hurtful words. You may be perceiving the situation through the filter of your identity fear. Ask for clarity.

One staff member regularly showed up late to our meetings. The head coach didn't punish him or scold him for being irresponsible. He was honest with him about how it made him feel and asked for a change in behavior: "When you show up late to our meetings I feel like you are taking advantage of our friendship."

The staff member reassured him that it wasn't out of disrespect and for the rest of the season he was early to every staff meeting. When you can ask for what you need with clarity it has the potential to deepen your relationships. If you model the outline for vulnerable communication for your team, you will set the standard of honesty that develops deep trust.

DEALING WITH ANGER

As you build your team, meet their needs, and lead with vulnerability, the journey won't be all sunshine and rainbows. Everyone on the team brings their unique struggles and insecurities. They all start with differing agendas. There will be a gap between what you see for them and where they are. All of that together will create the potential for conflict. Conflict isn't all bad, but how you handle it will determine the health of your team. Like the challenges you face in your individual pursuit, conflict can grow your team or erode your team.

ACKNOWLEDGING HOW YOUR DECISIONS MIGHT AFFECT OTHERS BUILDS TRUST THAT DEEPENS THE RELATIONSHIPS WITHIN YOUR TEAM.

At the root of conflict is an insecure person trying to meet the needs of their identity through others. When your insecurities ricochet off the insecurities of someone else, it produces conflict. Most often, that conflict is expressed through the emotion of anger.

Not all anger is bad. There is productive anger when it is stirred up by injustice or when it involves boundaries and protecting those you love. The desire to protect your home turf can be a righteous anger.

Not all anger is active. Passive anger spills over after burying the emotion over and over. It can be just as destructive. You will notice it in the forced, sterile responses, the eye rolls when they are subbed out of the game, and the resigned acceptance to decisions. They go with it but you can tell they haven't bought into it. If this anger isn't surfaced and dealt with, it will chip away at the health of your team and eventually combust.

Most coaches help athletes deal with anger by telling them to control their temper. This is a shallow response. It may or may not work in the short term, but it certainly doesn't address the deeper reality. Anger is often a surface-level response to a root-level experience of fear. It's the fear you learned about in the Relaxed Mindset. It's the fear that you won't get what your identity needs. Anger surfaces when you try to meet your needs through your mission or community and it doesn't work. Don't stop short by just controlling your temper. You have to process anger at a deeper level and understand what you feel you are lacking. If you can learn to do this quickly, you will be able to move on to the next play with minimal damage to your teammates or the flow of the game.

As a leader, how you respond to the anger within your team will shape how they process it. Turning up the pressure or increasing your intensity to get them to behave the way you want will only stir up more conflict. When you try to control their behavior, you become overly concerned with their performance and miss the opportunity to dig deeper into their identity and what is happening in their lives. It distracts you from equipping them with effective solutions. You could bully them into producing immediate results, but that approach neglects the healthy processes that lead to the long-term wins you are looking for.

Withdrawing yourself from others or treating them differently to communicate your displeasure is the passive approach to controlling their behavior. It's manipulative and just as destructive. Your athletes will feel the pain of the silent treatment but not have any effective solutions to change. They will lose trust in you and look elsewhere for leadership.

Anger is a tool of power. You can use it poorly to power up and take what you are lacking, or you can use it appropriately to protect yourself and others. You have to grow beyond the insecure need to constantly be validated. As a leader, you will put yourself out there and take risks. The problems you face and the humiliations you may experience will make you feel vulnerable, but you don't have to lash out from a stressed-out state. No external circumstance can steal your dignity and worth unless you

> ## ANGER IS A SURFACE-LEVEL RESPONSE TO A ROOT-LEVEL EXPERIENCE OF FEAR.

let it. You learned how to give yourself what you need with precision and accuracy. Now you will be able to give others the precise and accurate encouragement they need.

LOVE YOUR TEAM

When a player isn't responding to your coaching or the team isn't applying what you are teaching, take a deep breath and seek to understand. You can't lead well if you are frustrated. Their mistakes are not an attack on your identity. Remind yourself that you will be alright and seek clarity.

You don't have to give them a free pass on destructive behavior. You also don't have to communicate with them through shame or threats that make them feel bad about who they are. Affirm their personhood and then address their performance. Let them know you understand what they are experiencing, then focus on the action that needs to change. Name what they have done and explain how it negatively impacts them and the team. Consider what systems need to be created or changed to keep it from happening again. Is there relational toxicity that needs to be worked out? Is there misalignment on the vision, values, and strategies? If something isn't working you can ignore it, complain about it, or adjust. Be the kind of leader who adjusts.

AFFIRM PERSONHOOD AND THEN ADDRESS PERFORMANCE.

A team that can navigate conflict in a healthy way will develop an atmosphere of deep trust. Deep trust fuels the momentum of relationships. Team members will have the courage to take risks, be vulnerable, and develop themselves. The team won't lose itself in the extreme highs or lows of winning and losing. It will ground itself in the community that is being built. The team will stay connected through all the ups and downs of the season. You will weather them together.

On the whiteboard in my office I had one phrase written in green that survived all of the scribbling, erasing, and new ideas of the season:

Love your team.

The phrase wasn't about excusing all mistakes or ignoring all problems. It was a reminder that each player was on an individual journey to reach his best. It was a reminder that it wasn't about me. They needed help, and it was my job to meet them where they were and help them get to where they wanted to go.

The world needs more people with the ability to understand the other. It needs people who can serve and give love away even when being misunderstood. The Empathetic Mindset takes us the last mile of the human experience. Those who can develop it will have the opportunity to make the greatest impact on their communities.

EXERCISES TO DEVELOP AN EMPATHETIC MINDSET

1. Tear Down Your Pedestals

Model vulnerability by tearing down your pedestals. Even if you're not the head coach or the leading scorer, there are people in your community who hold you in high regard. What pedestal are you standing on because of your title, position, or role?

How can you tear down your pedestal?

2. Ask for What You Need

When you notice your insecurities flare up, ask for what you need with precision. Don't attack others in anger. You can't work with others well when you're frustrated. Instead of increasing your intensity, increase clarity. Seek understanding.

3. Manage Spacing

A leader fills space. A sage creates space. An empath meets space. You don't have to build your leadership around your strength while neglecting the other two. Develop your coaching style by improving your weaknesses and recognizing which role is needed and when. Use your strengths and spice up your coaching with the others.

Which of these roles is a strength for you?

Which of these roles is a weakness for you?

RELAXED
INTENSITY

When you began this journey, you were targeting the podium moment: cutting down the nets, kissing the trophy, receiving the gold medal. Unfortunately, results are never guaranteed. There isn't a performance hack or shortcut to glory. The hard work of chasing a championship can be as frustrating and unfruitful as trying to catch confetti fluttering to the floor. Even if you could catch it by the strength of your effort and willpower, you would discover that it doesn't satisfy what you truly desire.

The satisfaction you are looking for comes from a presence and state of mind that consistently positions you to experience joy and purpose; where fear and hesitation fades to the background; where time becomes irrelevant and you are lost in the moment; where performance is an overflow of who you are and the work you have put in; where you elevate an entire community, not just yourself.

It is Relaxed Intensity.

It's the perfect cocktail of the seven mindsets. It's where your greatest achievements are born, your growth accelerates, and the game breaks open.

Your attention is heightened and your skills are surrendered to instincts.

The voices of shame and fear are quieted. You are relaxed internally, with nothing to prove and nothing to hide. You have a non-anxious presence.

You have an intense focus. Fully present, fully engaged. Undistracted by false pressure.

It is just as valuable and enjoyable in the smallest encounters with friends and family as it is in the biggest championship moments.

Sarah Crouch placed third in the 25k race that was supposed to "kick her butt a little bit." After the race, she reflected on the experience of ditching her watch to race with her instincts and guts:

"This is what it feels like, I realized, to really live, to push myself to the very boundary of who I am and exist wholly in one moment without a thought or concern for the step I had just taken or the one I would take next. There was only the terrible and wonderful pain of now."

Some people have naturally acquired these mindsets through the environments they have been exposed to. Others have been forced into these mindsets to survive challenging circumstances. You don't have to wait for either of those to happen. The tools that can make the biggest difference in your life are not inaccessible resources. They are learnable skills and you have the capacity to learn them.

Cultivating and applying these mindsets will slowly transform you into a person who lives with the mind of a champion. It is not a linear process though. You will reach new heights and then be challenged by the vision of new horizons. You will open new doors and then be faced with the dark cave of uncharted territory. With every step forward, you will have to choose to upgrade your mindset and experience Relaxed Intensity in a new form.

Your pursuit and your relationships give meaning to your life, but they don't have to consume who you are. You are capable of doing work that improves the world. You are capable of loving people from a secure core. The mind matters in all of it. Neglecting the condition of your mindset will always leave you short of what could be. From now on, look for ways to upgrade your mindset. Look for ways to position yourself for experiences that relax fear, shed false pressures, affirm the best of who you are, harness the power of your practice, and invite others on your journey so you can fully appreciate the climb.

END NOTES

Resilient Mindset

Howes, L., 2018. Kobe Bryant: Mamba Mentality And The Mind Of A Champion. [podcast] The School of Greatness. Available at: <https://lewishowes.com/podcast/kobe-bryant-mamba-mentality-nba-championships-and-oscars/> [Accessed 29 May 2020].

The Last Dance, 2020. [TV program] ESPN: ESPN.

Relaxed Mindset

The nine identity fears grew out of contributions from fields of personality development and typology. This book was the initial spark:

Riso, D. and Hudson, R., 1999. The Wisdom Of The Enneagram. New York: Bantam Books.

BT Sport, 2018. Dressing Room Footage! Tyson Fury Consoles His Own Team-Mates After Controversial Draw. [video] Available at: <https://www.youtube.com/watch?v=rl-CvdqL3yY> [Accessed 29 May 2020].

Victor Mindset

USATF, 2018. Sarah Crouch Pre-Race - USATF 25 Km Championships 2018. [video] Available at: <https://www.usatf.tv/gprofile.php?mgroup_id=45365&mgroup_event_id=2514&year=2018&do=videos&video_id=242879> [Accessed 29 May 2020].

Waitzkin, J., 2007. The Art Of Learning. New York: Free Press, p.xxi, 43.

House of Highlights, 2018. Lebron James Postgame Interview - Game 2 | Cavaliers Vs Raptors | May 3, 2018 | 2018 NBA Playoffs. [video] Available at: <https://www.youtube.com/watch?v=SH5-Ay24wPU> [Accessed 29 May 2020].

My Next Guest Needs No Introduction with David Letterman, 2018. [TV program] Netflix: Netflix.

Eden, S., 2013. Stroke of madness. [Blog] ESPN, Available at: <https://www.espn.com/golf/story/_/id/8865487/tiger-woods-reinvents-golf-swing-third-career-espn-magazine> [Accessed 29 May 2020].

Howes, L., 2018. Kobe Bryant: Mamba Mentality And The Mind Of A Champion. [podcast] The School of Greatness. Available at: <https://lewishowes.com/podcast/kobe-bryant-mamba-mentality-nba-championships-and-oscars/> [Accessed 29 May 2020].

Atlas, T. and Alson, P., 2006. Atlas. New York, N.Y: HarperCollins Publishers, pp.170-173.

Relaxed Intensity

Crouch, S., 2018. Stigmata. [Blog] Sarah's Running Shorts, Available at: <https://sarahsrunningshorts.weebly.com/stigmata.html> [Accessed 29 May 2020].

For your next transformational experience, visit:

www.CatchingConfettiTheBook.com

Take your mindset to the next level with

1 on 1 coaching

Online video courses

Keynote speaking

Team events

Organization-wide training

Made in the USA
Monee, IL
06 April 2021